Lured by Mountains

By M.A. Harper

'Risk more than others think safe. Care more than others think is wise. Dream more than others think is practical. Expect more than others think is possible'.

Claude T. Bissell

Grosvenor House
Publishing Limited

This book is published by
Grosvenor House Publishing Ltd
Link House
140 The Broadway, Tolworth, Surrey, KT6 7HT.
www.grosvenorhousepublishing.co.uk

A CIP record for this book
is available from the British Library

ISBN 978-1-78623-049-2

Dedication

For Peter and Angus

with love and thanks for your support,
and to my mother who loved the mountains of Switzerland.

CONTENTS

Preface

M.A. was born and brought up in Edinburgh. She spent a year at school in Switzerland, where she was introduced to skiing and climbing. Returning to Edinburgh she trained as a secretary and in this role she worked in Germany and America before taking off and travelling alone across the US. After a few wild adventures in the mountains of the Rockies she ended up back in Scotland, and trained to be a ski instructor. She also met up with a group of superb technical climbers, one of whom, Fred Harper, would become her husband. She started life as Marjorie-Anne, but this was soon dropped by her friends in favour of 'M.A.' by which name she has been known ever since.

She went to University, feeling she had missed out on education, and took a degree in Fine Art in 1967, before abandoning it all to drive to India with her husband and two others to climb a previously unclimbed peak in the Himalayas.

Returning to Scotland to live at Glenmore Lodge where her husband was the principal, she later on had two sons, Peter and Angus, and it was only after her marriage unravelled that she became a qualified outdoor instructor, teaching skiing, kayaking and sailing to children on Loch Insh in Speyside. She led walking weeks in Scotland and for a short time ran her own walking business, *Freespirit*. Thereafter she found work as a trek leader and travelled with groups to Nepal, Morocco, Greece, Russia, Spain and the Alps. She also fulfilled her own ambitions and climbed the Matterhorn and Mount Kenya, and walked in Patagonia, Ecuador and Bolivia. She also backpacked in America and completed the John Muir Trail on the day of 9/11. She was made a Fellow of the Royal Geographical Society in 2009 on election by Fellow friends. She was also a member of the Ladies Scottish Climbing Club and made many interesting friends.

M.A. completed the Munros in 1996, mostly solo, and then completed the Challenge walk across Scotland seven times. During several summers she has worked with the National Trust and has been lucky enough to go to both St Kilda and Fair Isle on work parties. Holidays have been biking in India and Cuba, and sea kayaking in Scotland and the Lofotens. In 2016 she fulfilled a dream and went south to the Antarctic to see the penguins and to South Georgia to pay homage to Shackleton.

Stepping back for a few years she pursued photography in Edinburgh and won a gold award, but this has now taken a back seat. She now has five grandchildren and feels she is moving more and more into the role of enjoying them and following their adventures.

Though she still has plans...

Where are you going?

Where are you going? Nowhere, I said,
Up to the mountains to clear my head.

Why are you going? What does it matter?
Away from the world of bustle and clatter.

What will you do, when you get there?
I'll take a deep breath of wonderful air.

Why do you want to fly so high?
To watch the clouds float over the sky.

Why are your feet so itchy to move?
For fear they stick in a mundane groove.

Why are you here, so far from the city?
Mortals below are worthy of pity.

Why can't you sit and enjoy the sun?
A lotus-eater has little fun.

And man – if he really wants to survive –
Must always be doing, to stay alive.

Can you not be? Why must you do?
Why can't you sit and enjoy the view?

A man will rot if he stays quite still,
He must always see what's over the hill.

Won't you just wait and rest for a day.
Sorry, I can't for I'm on my way.

James Thin (1923–97)

CHAPTER ONE
Introduction

Starting Out

'I hang on to the strong steel spike at the top of the fixed ropes. It is so solid, can I just stay here? Some people are already descending. I cannot stay here…I let go of the spike and its security, and place a cramponed foot on the hard snow névé of the slope below the summit. A precarious spot this, as the ground falls away 5,000ft to the glaciers below…I am making my way to the summit of the Matterhorn, fulfilling a dream I had nurtured for over half a century.'

I reflect on where all this wild adventuring came from – this need to be high up – that was later to take over my life as I climbed and roamed the mountains of the world.

One of my earliest memories, from 50 years previously, is of following my father up on to the top of the four-storey tenement building near Bruntsfield, in Edinburgh, where I lived as a child. Aged five, it just seemed too exciting a chance to ignore, and up I went. When I emerged through the skylight window on to the flat rooftop I had great views of surrounding gardens and it was thrilling being close to the chimney pots! My father was very shocked to find me behind him; aghast, he showed me the way back down the ladder.

My father had been in the First World War and even survived the Battle of the Somme. He had been a friend of my grandfather, and my mother persuaded him to marry her. He was 44 when I was born, my mother was 32. He had had two brothers, who died young, but I never learnt more and his family life with a lawyer father in the west of Scotland had been less than fun. He had attended Watson's College in Edinburgh as a boy, aged nine. All this was a closed book, as he never spoke of any of his previous life. I think life in the trenches and an unhappy childhood must have damaged him a great deal and he did not really want children, so I remained an only child.

When I was ten my mother finally managed to persuade my father to buy a house with a garden, and so we moved there. I was desperate

1

Me and cat

for a dog and wanted a Shetland sheepdog, but this was not to be. They bought a Sealyham, which learnt to beg and went for short walks with my father, so I still had no dog.

Although my parents sent me to a private girls' school and gave me what they must have hoped would be the foundations of a firm future, I was a rebellious child. The expectations of a conventional Edinburgh upbringing in a lawyer's family in the 1940s and 50s were hugely at variance with what I imagined I wanted, though I was not sure what that was. Somehow at school it is important to fit in so I did all the right things – playing tennis and hockey for the school, learning to play bridge – but my heart was not in it. In fact I was always aware of having to be careful of money and felt marked out by my school uniform, which was handed down from a friend of my parents; this was very hard. I went to dances and balls, and even the May Ball at Clare College, Cambridge. I felt very inferior there; I had sewn my own ball gown but was surrounded by smart London girls in swish bouncy dresses.

School was a prison to me and I was happiest at the weekends when I escaped into the freedom of fresh air with the wind in my hair, and hills and emptiness around me.

My weekends were spent near Glasgow with my mother's parents who had a large house with a huge garden and an orchard near the River

Clyde at Uddingston. There I was able to indulge my need for freedom. Peter, the Labrador, waited as I opened the car door when we arrived, and together we would head off down to the Clyde to explore. My grandmother had ducks and hens and I collected blue-green eggs from under various bushes, smelling the dry hay of the nests. I even learnt to ride Rosy, a vast Clydesdale horse with huge pink nostrils and long eye-lashes, belonging to the farmer next door. My legs would barely strad-dle her back as I clung on bareback, hanging on to her mane, burying my nose in her smelly, brown coat as we swung across the fields with Peter bouncing along behind. At the stables out at Colinton I groomed my adopted pony, Mousie, and led people out on rides.

Holidays in the early days, about 1946, were taken in a guesthouse at Elie on the Fife Coast. Having no companion, I spent the days digging big holes in the beach and the evenings drawing pictures of boats with the help of a fellow visitor in the guesthouse.

When I was twelve we went to Newtonmore in the Spey Valley. This journey from Edinburgh took the whole day then and we would have a picnic somewhere near Pitlochry, sitting in a field with a thermos

Mother and father

3

and sandwiches. My father called the main road north 'The Great North Lane'. It was a slow road and we had a slow car – an Austin Eight.

My parents played golf during the day but they did hire a Highland Pony, Molly, for me during the time I was there, so I spent many happy days riding on my own in the hills. I loved the freedom and the pleasure of being with my pony. Sometimes I swam in the River Calder and looked for fish, which were a bit scary.

For some reason I was also reading all I could on Tibet and the Dalai Lama, Heinrich Harrer's book, *Seven Years in Tibet*, plus of course his climbing book, *White Spider*, about the ascent of the Eiger North Face. I do not think I ever imagined I would climb the North Face, but I was there in spirit, and felt the ice on my eye lashes and frozen fingers on the rope, as I shared the ascents, my hot breath forming icicles on my scarf.

My great uncle Alec, who was a doctor and became superintendent of the Royal Infirmary in Edinburgh in 1935, was a big influence too. I discovered that in 1931, when he had been working in India as the Director of Public Health at the Institute of All India Public Health and Hygiene, he was at an Officers' Club and heard of an expedition to Tibet, so he said, "Well you will need a doctor". He went, and I have his Tibetan Prayer Wheel still. Imagine going to Tibet in 1931!

However, my mother had been fortunate to go to school in Switzerland for a year and had a passion for mountains. She was determined I should also have this chance.

When I was 17, I boarded a train from Edinburgh bound for London, a ferry over the Channel, (being sick all the way), and then a train for Lausanne on the edge of Lake Geneva in Switzerland. Amazing now to think that I wore my tweed coat with a silk scarf tied under my chin, which was our uniform as educated young ladies! I ended up in Gstaad at a school called Montesano, in the mountains above Lausanne where there were about 150 girls, some very young and following the baccalaureate education system, for this was not officially a 'finishing school' for everyone.

Some pupils were very sophisticated and aristocratic; one was going out with the Aga Khan who was also at school in Gstaad. Another was Caroline Abel Smith, whose mother was, I think, lady-in-waiting to the Queen. I met some wonderful American girls, Italian girls and a variety of girls from Britain, including a good friend, Jane Harrison, from Edinburgh. I shared a room with four others, and found the companionship so stimulating and such fun after my solitary times in Edinburgh.

I learnt to ski here and fell in love with skiing, but my happiest moments were spent with two friends and our handsome instructor, Charles Louis, scrambling up local crags. One of these was called Les Trois Pucelles, which translates as The Three Virgins, but this meaning escaped me at the time! This was a wonderful free time, full of company and fresh air when three of us were off climbing every possible weekend. I was supposed to climb the Matterhorn that summer of 1958, but had to come home in order to be presented to the Queen at the last Presentation at Holyrood. This was the last thing I wanted but I felt I owed it to my mother who had planned it. I did work very hard on my French and passed Higher Prelim French on my return, so validating my time away. I waited until 1994 when I was 54 to climb the Matterhorn, some dreams never die!

My great uncle Will was a vet in Blairgowrie, and I wanted so much to be a vet myself, but this was not encouraged. In desperation my parents packed me off to Dugdale's Secretarial College for a year of training. For an outdoor adventurer this was simply another prison! In hindsight I can see that in 1958 one did what one was told, like it or not.

However, I passed my exams with good speeds in shorthand and typing and joined my friend Rosie in Oxford, where I worked in a law office. I hated being imprisoned in an airless room tapping away at a typewriter facing a blank wall and so did not enjoy Oxford at all, spending much time beagling and punting on my own. I think being an only child made it difficult for me to share affection and to break down the boundaries between people, so that I seemed to be essentially more confident in my own company. Rosie was very popular and good fun and so we did have some charming young men come to drink coffee at the flat. Part of the summer ritual was the lunchtime Pimm's parties on the river. I would cycle slightly woozily back to the office in my tight skirt and my fingers would hop over the keys of the typewriter to produce another conveyance, but no one seemed to mind.

My father found an advert in *The Scotsman* for a law firm in Cologne, which was looking for an English secretary and I applied. I was interviewed in Edinburgh, and took the job, despite my misgivings that there were no hills nearby. I flew out first class and drank some champagne to fortify myself. I did not speak German, had never been to Germany and had not yet met my boss, Dieter, for whom I was to work. The work, in a prestigious law firm dealing with trademarks, was hard and Dieter was daunting and tireless; he was half Japanese and half German and his working day knew no limits.

I worked from eight in the morning till eight at night and until four on a Saturday. The plan was that I would improve the language and syntax of Dieter's letters in English to the Americans. I took pages and pages of shorthand, sometimes as many as 45, and in between this I wrote letters in French for another member of the staff who was working for the new EEC in Brussels. Our high profile clients in the States included Johnson and Johnson and Pfizer and as my German became more fluent, so my English letters became less flowing.

I did buy a car and in what free time I had was able to go off to the countryside, and to Amsterdam.

Trying to go walking in this place was impossible; I had little free time so that I could only get out on a Sunday if I took a tram at 5 a.m. to join a local Alpine Club. I only went once as at that point I was 21 and they all seemed very old and we walked through the woods.

So I gave up and joined my German workmate, Usch, and her considerably younger friends who liked to go on pub crawls on Saturdays. Dress and hairstyles seemed to be the important things so I did not really fit in here. But it seemed very difficult to meet people in Cologne.

My accommodation, a bedsit in a flat with a couple whose one child was locked in her room by a gate during the day, was impossible. I could not cook there and lived on yogurt, liver pate and gherkins, so if I was invited out I ate steak!

Finally, after fourteen months of this unrelenting and boring way of life I left and retreated home. The home I returned to was not home as I had left it because my grandparents were now also living there. My mother was much occupied with them and so I had a bit of a breakdown.

In 1963 I took off for the US and worked in New York for a month, finding work in a typing pool with one of our clients whom I had met in Cologne. I stayed in a smart apartment belonging to a friend I had met at Montesano and saved my pennies to buy a Ninety Nine Dollar ticket for the Greyhound bus and travelled across America. I never looked back!

I had a great time, travelling on the bus to the Midwest, climbing in Colorado, walking down to the river in the Grand Canyon with a Frenchman I met on the bus, with no water, just a gin and tonic at the end. I then travelled down to Texas and Mexico to meet Ian from Edinburgh. We were four in a car and we went on down to Acapulco, where I tried body surfing in huge waves that dumped me on the rough sand and skinned my tummy. I walked along the beach one day and clad only in my swimwear and a shirt, hitched a ride with three men in a car. When they stopped outside a hotel laughing and babbling in Spanish, I got out. I think I was lucky, foolish and naive, but lucky. Times are different now and in 2016 one would not risk anything so silly.

I returned to Scotland and in 1963, worked briefly in London, during which time John F. Kennedy was shot. But London life was not for me, and while working for Columbia Pictures, I glanced at the paper and saw that the Youth Hostel Association was looking for ski instructors. This was too tempting, and I abandoned London and the office in favour of Glen Isla and the Youth Hostel, which I hoped would transform my future and turn me into a ski instructor. At Glen Isla I met Pam, who had taught skiing and riding in Chile, and after much laughter and many tumbles into the heather, we qualified as ski instructors.

I taught skiing for two seasons at Loch Morlich Youth Hostel in the Cairngorms earning £6.14s a week. I loved the life, the snow, the cold, the challenges and the company and found it all wrong to be paid to be outside all day enjoying myself.

In 1963 things were very informal on the hill; we all knew one another, there was only one chairlift to take us up the mountain, and then a mad race to book the best site for teaching by sticking your skis in a patch of snow in the heather. On Friday nights we 'repaired' the wooden skis, replacing the metal edges if possible, otherwise we just painted them with the red lead we used to cover the scratches. It was astonishing that anyone actually managed to learn to ski using leather boots and these long skis which often had a 'reverse camber', so that they rose at each end instead of in the middle where the spring should be.

It seems amazing that in those days there were actually eight ski schools in the Cairngorms because each village had its own school. In the evenings, as the nights lengthened we played games with the students, sometimes there was tree climbing or football on the sand at Loch Morlich. We had our own ceilidhs at the Hostel, but often drove down to a ceilidh or folk singing in one of the Aviemore hotels.

Life on the hill in winter weather could be painfully harsh. Many years later Harry Jamieson, with whom I taught skiing on Cairngorm, recalled an incident on the hill. The weather closed in and the chairlift staff requested that everyone should leave the hill. I was frozen and approached Harry's van pleading for a lift, "No sooner had MA entered the vehicle, bringing snow with her, than she started weeping with pain, as her feet were frozen in her plastic boots, and she could not get them off. When we got her feet out she placed both on my warm stomach to thaw out. The crying got louder, from both of us, and to this day I think I can see size five feet on my chest". This seemed funny at the time but I later read that this was what they did with Scott in the Antarctic, a time tested remedy.

We were not far from Glenmore Lodge and as we were short on creature comforts, we gladly accepted the offers of hot showers and invitations to dinner there with the Principal Eric Langmuir and his wife Maureen. While there I met Joe Brown, (of climbing fame) who regularly brought students to the Cairngorms. Joe's students were housed in huts, which had been used by the Kompani Linge in the 1940s. These Norwegian soldiers had trained in mountain warfare in the Cairngorms where the terrain provided good preparation for carrying out acts of sabotage back in their German occupied homeland. Joe and I planned to climb a snow gully together but this never worked out.

During this time I decided to go to University and, after days teaching skiing on the hill, worked hard to get my German Higher. I went to Edinburgh University intending to study for French and German honours, but my German had no depth, and no literature, so I floundered and changed to Fine Art and Sociology. Later, following my marriage, I transferred to Glasgow for my honours year, but the commute from Argyll where we were then living, was stressful and put a strain on the marriage and despite loving researching into Italian architecture and painting, I reluctantly gave up my Honours year and took the ordinary M.A.

In the summer following the skiing, I had toured the mountains of Austria with my friend, Pam. During our trip Pam and I slept in old cabins, including on one occasion a climbing hut where at dawn we heard the clatter of 'gear' being put together – ropes being coiled, carabiners clicking and clattering together on the floor in the dark. I had not climbed since leaving Switzerland in 1958 but this was to prove another transformational experience, firing me with the ambition to get back into climbing.

Back in Edinburgh and eagerly seeking out the climbing community, I was directed firstly to Graham Tiso's climbing shop at the east end of Princes Street. Graham told me to introduce myself to the 'Squirrels', a group of climbers who met each week in the Wee Windaes pub on the High Street. This was intimidating; I found myself the only woman amidst the burly climbers but, since I had a car and could help with transport on a Friday night to Glencoe, I was made welcome.

I climbed with the Squirrels regularly, picking them up from Binns corner (now House of Fraser) at the west end of Princes Street. Bugs McKeith, the youngest of the group and regarded with some suspicion by the 'hard men', took me up a few routes on Buchaille Etive Mor. I was still climbing in my rubber soled leather ski boots but we managed Agag's Groove and Crowberry Ridge, and before climbing Revelation, then considered to be the hard one. I think that it was Bug's quiet announcement, met with stunned silence, that we had just climbed Revelation that led to my acceptance by the Squirrels.

The Squirrels base was the Drey, a structure on the hillside above the gorge. Here, after a few beers in the bar at the Clachaig Inn, the language would become pretty colourful and I was sometimes treated a bit rudely, but stuck it out for the sake of the climbing. My mother was rather dismayed that I went off every weekend with a lot of men, sharing a sleeping shelf in the Drey or even worse – one tent. However, I was with the top climbers in Scotland at the time and had found what would change the course of my life.

The Squirrels were active in putting up new routes all over Scotland. Fred, who was to become my future husband, was a member of this elite group. We sometimes climbed with Dougal Haston and his girlfriend Joy; Hamish McInnes intended to, but never did, make a film of us climbing.

The Squirrels' forerunners had been the Creag Dhu Club whose members came mostly from Glasgow and the docks. They were strong, hard men whom I was to meet later in Aviemore where some of them drifted into jobs connected with the booming ski industry on Cairngorm. Bob Clyde ran the Chairlift Company; others worked at Glenmore Lodge or set up ski schools.

Fred and I climbed a lot then – in Scotland, Wales and the Lake District. Further afield we climbed in the Dolomites and down near Marseilles on the sea cliffs, called the Calanques. It was there that, one night as I lay outside under the pines, I encountered Don Whillans who tripped over me leaving his sandal behind. Don and Joe Brown were well known at that time for the new routes they had 'put up' on cliffs everywhere. In 1968 we went to the Alps and completed a Traverse of Mont Maudit, Mont Blanc de Tacul, and Mont Blanc, descending by the normal route of ascent. In those days the summit of Mont Blanc was deserted.

These twin passions, skiing and climbing and my involvement with the extraordinary group of dedicated devotees of the sports became the driving forces that were to shape my future.

Fred and I lived at Benmore Centre in Argyll, an outdoor centre run by Edinburgh Council, where my husband taught climbing (as did I) at the weekends. In 1968 we drove across Europe, Turkey, Iran, Afghanistan and Pakistan to India in order make the first ascent of Ali Ratni Tibba in the north of India.

On our return Fred took a job at Marlborough College for a time before being offered the job of Deputy at Glenmore Lodge near Aviemore. I knew the Principal, Eric Langmuir, his wife Mo, and their growing family well, having spent many happy hours in their flat at the Lodge in the 60s while I was teaching skiing. I had come full circle and was back near Loch Morlich and the Cairngorms and in 1970 Fred took over from Eric as Principal.

I had two sons, Peter and Angus, and a fairly happy life, though there were no other children at the Lodge in those days. My children grew up listening to helicopters landing outside the window as they came for rescues or training. The helicopters sounded as if they were coming through the ceiling into our sitting room, it must have been so scary for the poor boys who clung to my trouser legs in terror. As a young mother I was exhausted and isolated at the Lodge with no other mothers and children and so became very depressed.

Fred and I both loved climbing and art and had lots in common. Like most climbers of the time, he regarded skiers as 'penguins', but after a few bad winter climbing seasons (of no snow and less ice) he became a skier too. I was passionate about skiing and although I did some winter climbing, I found that sitting in a sunless, cold gully waiting to climb, was not nearly as exciting as swooping down a sunny slope on skis.

Fred and I parted company in 1981. I lived locally, and tried to do my best for Peter and Angus, who shortly went off to prep school and then to Gordonstoun, where their best friends were already installed.

My mother, who was living on her own in Edinburgh, developed Alzheimer's. By then I was leading treks, she needed care and I found I could not provide it, nor could I cope. I did try to arrange for various carers to come, but they would take one look at my hyperactive mother and not stay. I continued to lead treks at this time, but always covered my absence by arranging help and telling the doctors and lawyers that I was away for a month. The trekking company, Sherpa, was really helpful and knew how I was placed and worked with me... Exodus who had a business to run, were unable to be so accommodating. I found a Home in Inverness which would take my mother...and when I was in Nepal I had a telegram from my son, Peter, saying that a vacancy had come up and he was taking her to Inverness. I would have found that so difficult. She never asked for home and never went home again. The best thing at this time was, that although she was unable to speak, I grew much closer to my mother. Her face glowed with joy when she saw me, she held out her hand to me, and mouthed 'wonderful'. This was a good time, and I was glad I had it with her.

Eventually my mother fell down the stairs in the Home and broke her leg and really this marked the road to the end. She was in hospital in Inverness for three months, during which time I visited every day and we tried to encourage her to walk. Her eyes would shine with determination but, aged 85, walking was beyond her. I then had to find her a different Home, where she died on New Year's Eve 1993, waiting to see Peter and Angus, who had hurried home from France where they were with their father, before she let go, I remember them sitting on either side of her bed, then the next day while I was with her, she stopped breathing.

It was Hogmanay. The boys had offered to come home to be with me, but I told them that I would be fine and that they should enjoy their New Year's Eve parties. This was a bad plan; I was invited out for a meal but broke down in the middle, and had to go home.

As I grew up I was influenced by contacts with wildness and the outdoors and was attracted to challenges, which led me to take off into the world on my own. They drew me to those twin passions, skiing and climbing to which I came in my early adulthood. Together with my involvement in the extraordinary group of dedicated devotees of the sports, they became the driving forces that were to shape my life. I became a 'mountain person', one of a close-knit group of individuals described thus by my friend, Harry Jamieson, with whom I taught on Cairngorm. "M.A. Harper…first of all she was a mountain person, one of us, by that I mean, someone who lived at a certain time at Glenmore, in the sixties to the eighties, and in a community with a climate and weather like no other place in Britain. These people were hard and close, and they would give you anything you required, whether it was during the day or in the middle of the night…all totally committed to safety and pleasure".

CHAPTER TWO

Personal Goals and Travels

Driving to India, Part 1: Benmore to Persia, April 1969

The 15,000-mile journey to India, there and back, across so many countries took us 21 days, driving for 12 hours a day. We didn't think too much about it, Fred and the others (Jim McCartney, who tragically was killed by an avalanche on Ben Nevis in January 1970 and Dave Nicol) were focussed on climbing Ali Ratni Tibba in Himachal Pradesh, in the north of India.

Mountaineering magazines had described Ali Ratni Tibba as 'A splendid ice and granite obelisk' and it had been attempted twice unsuccessfully, in 1961 and 1965. W.H. Murray, the mountaineer and author, had kindly agreed to be our patron, lending an air of seriousness and respectability to our trip. Dave, Fred and I all worked at Benmore Adventure Centre in Argyll, taking children up into the hills and canoeing on the loch. Chris worked as a sales manager for Tube Investments and was a great asset, being good at lists and sub lists. The trip had been four years in the planning, and I had written many begging letters for food and equipment resulting in sundry returns, new jerseys for us, a box of Weetabix, Vesta Beef Curry, tins of haggis and Mars bars, which unfortunately arrived too late. We were fortunate to be given a substantial gift from the Mount Everest Foundation, some money from the Gannochy Trust and cheques from two Scottish Banks. Even with this level of support we were mainly funded from our own pockets and we could not afford to fly ourselves there. Fortunately we were also part given a short wheelbase Ford Transit van, so four of us drove out and were joined later by Chris who flew out. The van would need to be serviced in Ankara, Tehran, Kabul and Delhi, it was worrying that no one would insure our van for this wild journey, so we just had to trust to luck.

We had divided the inside of the van into three parts, an arrangement that worked well. The front was for the driver and passenger, the middle section was floored with boxes of food and partitioned off from

13

the back, which was stacked high with climbing gear and tents. On the tins of food we had laid a sheet of cardboard covered with a layer of foam. Two people would lie there for three hours while one drove and the third passenger sat by the driver until taking over. There were no windows in the side of the van so whilst lying on the tins one could only read or sleep, but I passed the time in the front seat by knitting.

Incredible as it now seems, we drove through London where we collected Afghani visas, Jim had a haircut in Piccadilly, and we went to Harrods to buy smoked salmon.

We crossed the Channel, collected ropes from the Salewa Company near Munich then sat on the pavement by the parked van to eat our breakfast of fresh bread and jam with coffee cooked up on a camping stove. We then drove through Austria into Yugoslavia where we were amazed to see farmers working the fields with wooden ploughs and oxen. In a bar in Belgrade we breakfasted – this time on roast pork, kidneys, schnitzels and *Raznickhji* (pork kebabs), washed down with beer. There we drank wonderful sweet thick coffee served in little copper pots, which I have still.

Istanbul, in Turkey, marked progress. It was thronged with travellers, following the then crowded 'hippie trail', many of them moving by bus across Afghanistan and Pakistan to India. There I was offered, but refused, a highly fashionable Afghan coat, worth about £12 in exchange for my valuable Voigtlander camera. The Istanbul markets selling figs, prunes and olives alongside strange flat fish, had a bitter and astringent smell. The open meat shops with lungs hung up by the windpipe and braided intestines hanging outside seemed exotic to us. We did actually buy an old pistol, which I think we felt would protect us somehow on our long journey. In Istanbul we visited the Blue Mosque, inside were the blue and red tiles for which it is named. The floor was covered in rugs, and we left our shoes in a box at the foot of a pillar. My knee length skirt attracted so much attention that we abandoned our intention to visit the sixth century Sancta Sophia, one of the greatest Byzantine constructions in the world.

As we headed north to the Black Sea coast I was shocked by seeing the men walking unburdened by the side of women and donkeys, both heavily laden with milk churns or piles of wood. The local houses were built from handmade bricks and sticks and all the carts had wooden wheels. Swifts dived and swooped around us, while the roadsides were piled high with oranges, onions and mountains of leeks. There is a local tradition of looking after travellers and at Samsun, later that evening, we were very touched by a wee boy turning up at our campsite bringing us a tray on which were an omelette, a bowl of yoghurt and some cherries.

After dark the next evening, when the boys were bedded down on the ground outside the van, and Fred was cooking his haggis, two cars rolled up. One car turned round and drove off down the hill, the other one stopped and put out its lights. A fellow in uniform got out and said, "Turkish Police" and passed some cigarettes round, before shaking our hands and getting back into the car. He roared off down the hill emptying his pistol out of the window. We felt very vulnerable.

We climbed up into the Soganli Dag in the Kackar Mountains, through passes of over 6,000ft in a wild, rocky land of red rock pinnacles, plunging gullies, and snow-capped peaks. In place of the primulas and speedwells of the Black Sea, here there were crocuses, juniper and scrubby vegetation, which provided grazing for strange brown sheep with spindly legs. Here in Kurdistan, the men wore turbans and the women were hidden behind *burkas*. Their houses had mud walls and flat, grass roofs that merged with the hillside and were guarded by huge lurking dogs the size of bears. Paths wound round the houses, through low broken walls and donkeys, cows, sheep and hens wandered about at will.

Later we descended into wide flat plains, vast and open with the huge cone of Mount Ararat rising to 17,000ft above them. The larks singing shrilly overhead know no boundaries but the heavy military presence signalled how close we were to Russia, with Armenia just over the border. We approached Customs, which was shared with Persia, (now Iran) and, although in a modern concrete building, it was inconceivably filthy, dirty, unkempt and almost abandoned, as I have learnt since, the usual manner of the Customs areas of no man's land.

We then entered what was then called Persia, the Shah having remained in power until 1979, but is now Iran.

By this time it was 10 p.m. and having been driving since 4 a.m., we were pretty tired and were glad to be directed to a hotel. We hoped for a wash and some food, but being shown, by two filthy local men, into a

shabby empty room, we looked at one another with resignation. The Shah
and his wife, the Farah Diba, looked down on us out of a broken picture
frame and a chandelier hung precariously over our heads. We were
directed to a 'pond' in the yard to wash, where a man bent into a hole in
the ground to turn on a tap, which dribbled some more indescribably
filthy water into a sink submerged in the 'pond'. After our wash we
refreshed our spirits with Persian vodka and Coca Cola, but when our
kebabs arrived on a bed of rice they tasted very 'off' so I left mine.
Turkish champagne finished us for the night and we slept soundly.

Next day we continued driving on appalling roads, pitted with potholes and corrugations. The villages were mud houses surrounding
orchards of blossoming fruit trees, such flashes of colour amid an otherwise arid, featureless landscape. My excitement at suddenly seeing a
herd of cattle, camels and donkeys, was so great that I nearly drove off
the road.

We then approached Tehran, situated at an altitude of 3,700ft
against the backdrop of the snow-capped Elbruz Mountains and surrounded by magnificent countryside. We drove through a plain scattered with small herds of brown sheep and goats, on both sides were
hazy, blue mountains with the 19,600ft of Mount Demavend looming
above the hot blue haze. So much has changed in the interim, although I
expect the sheep and camels remain.

In Tehran we had wonderful breakfast of *lavash* (bread), omelette,
and coffee in a cafe where there were other Westerners. Here, much to
my relief, I was not stared at; being the only woman in our vehicle I was
sick and tired of being the focus of male attention all the time.

While the van was being serviced we had lots of time to fill, so Fred
and I went into the Bazaar. This was a fantastic place where men were
beating out copper pots and the cornucopia of merchandise on offer
included rugs, saddle bags, spices, seeds, antiques, inlaid boxes from
Shiraz, silverwork from Isfahan, tea, sweets, water bottles, shoes, towels
and Afghan jackets. I bought a fairly large glorious red tribal rug for £8.

We had a good time here, a welcome break from driving. I still
remember where we had lunch, the recommended *Chelokebab*. We got
a taxi to a restaurant the driver knew, which despite the partridges
pecking round the floor, was indeed grand, with a doorman at the
entrance and a large chandelier in the middle. What the smart waiters

and the prosperous looking locals dining at clean tables thought of four scruffy travellers I neither knew nor cared. Not having had a square meal since we left Benmore, we decided to 'go for it' and forget the cost, which was actually the same as breakfast. We had a large plate of Caspian rice with a generous knob of butter in it, mixed through with a raw egg yolk, salt and pepper and spice. This was followed by two lamb steak kebabs accompanied by grilled tomatoes and eaten with raw carrots, onions, pickled cauliflower, gherkins and yoghurt, with curry sauce. All this was washed down by *Dugh,* a drink made of yoghurt and mineral water. We felt much revived by this whole experience, a complete change from heating up a tin of haggis by the roadside or visiting a suspect hole in the wall.

Next day we drove north over the Elbruz Mountains along a road frequently destroyed by landslides. We saw bread being baked in a mud oven in the ground by people who appeared to be desperately poor. Their mud houses had straw roofs and were built close together to form a square with an impenetrable wall connecting them. It seemed a hostile place.

For about 280 miles we bounced along a road consisting of gravel and potholes. We were overtaken by a *dolmus,* one of the minibuses that stop everywhere here to pick up passengers. This particular one was going at about 60 mph. and had six untethered sheep on the roof, sitting on the rack behind the luggage. We stopped to allow a caravan of about a hundred camels, plus young, to pass us. One of the adult camels had its calf strapped to its back, other camels carried donkeys, foals or children also strapped on top. This extraordinary sight was followed by a large flock of sheep, tended by the women.

We reached Meshed, the stronghold of the *Mullahs,* the religious fanatics of the time, who wore green turbans, and fanned the flames of Muslim superiority; even at that time they were much feared. Everywhere we moved the crowd swarmed round the van and, as my diary recorded, *"they lean in the window frames and laugh at me and gaped...I am now buttoned to the neck and the ankle, but it makes no difference. Of course it's natural when all women are covered up and unseen and they rarely see a foreigner from Teheran far less Europe, but I have had enough."* I hated this and close to tears had to almost be locked in the van.

Driving to India Part Two: Persia to Afghanistan, Pakistan and India, April 1969

After our time in what was then Persia, now Iran, Afghanistan seemed like a breath of fresh air, we were delighted to have left the bone and van shaking potholes of the Persian roads behind us. We were now in a wide sweeping desert studded with black nomad tents, grazing camels, herds of white and brown sheep, and with flocks of brightly coloured small birds. We spent the night camped in the no man's land by the Customs before stopping, in search of petrol, at a small house where the bus usually comes in after Customs. Fred and I went in through an open doorway and were met by a little gnome-like man who took my hand and motioned us to sit on the mats on the floor where he served us teapots, sugar and glasses. When we had drunk our tea we shook hands and left whereupon the gnome-like man chased after us with our change of one shilling!

We drove through the ancient city of Herat, where Alexander the Great had founded a colony around 300 BC. Little remained of the town's original tiling but four outstanding minarets still rose above the rooftops. The main street was lined with bushy needled pine trees and all manner of booths displaying pelts, jackets and rugs. There were little booths which sold a huge array of goods and where little Astrakhan hats were made and butchers and potters plied their trades. The scent of freshly baked bread wafted teasingly right down the street from the underground ovens where it was baked. The bread was formed into flat loaves – moulded on a large leather cushion, then smacked against the edge of the hot, chimney shaped oven – eaten hot and crisp it was delicious.

We felt relaxed here as, unlike in Persia or Turkey, there was no begging or fawning, just a discreet, dignified aloofness. The Afghan men had long prophet-like beards and were shrouded in loose white trousers, tunic shirts, and Western jackets. On their heads they each wore a multi-coloured hat with a large turban wound round it, behind the turban hung a long tail of cloth which was used to cover the mouth when on the dusty roads. The women wore the *burka,* a complete cap, cloak and face covering with only a lace-covered slit over the eyes to allow the wearer to see. These women floated along – ghostlike. We were amazed at the white teeth of all the men and children, presumably a result of a diet rich in yogurt and camel's milk but devoid of sugar.

From Herat to Kandahar we followed the concrete road built by the Russians through a scorching desert, totally empty apart from occasional nomads and camels. On a fellow traveller's recommendation we were looking for the Farahrod Hotel, the stopping-off place between Herat and Kandahar. The hotel boasted fifty bedrooms, a swimming pool with changing booths and two springboards. Alas, the lawns were mangy, the flowerbeds weed ridden and littered with broken glass, the reception desk was deserted and there were no guests. The hotel kitchen was situated in a wooden shack over the wall from the main compound. We camped by the pool and were served with rice and eggs delivered to us by a waiter who climbed over the wall using a rickety ladder! This was our first rest day since leaving Scotland over two weeks earlier, and since it was so hot that a candle melted on the ground, we spent it in a leisurely way – reading, sunbathing and swimming in the slightly murky water of the pool.

Next day we were up at 5 a.m. and off on the flat concrete road again, leaving the mountains behind us as we continued towards Kandahar. We treated ourselves to tea in the garden of the Kandahar Hotel. The garden must have been well watered – conifers, snapdragons, geraniums, oleander, pansies and phlox flourished there. Whilst jays screeched in the trees, I luxuriated in the abundance of colour after the miles of dry, sandy, barren desert.

We were now heading towards Kabul. It was very dry and the wind blew the silt from the riverbed to form spirals and clouds. The American built asphalt road to Kabul was thronged with nomads and little boys with herds of sheep and goats, camels, donkeys with foals, old men with white beards and wrinkled black faces and deep sunken eyes. We were still meeting fantastic 'cattle lorries' – gaily painted wagons decorated with mirrors and ribbon and with piles of sheep and people on top and with people hanging off the back.

Unable to find anywhere to camp, we spent a night at the roadside and were astonished to awake to rain. We were now 6,207 miles from Benmore and had been driving for seventeen days.

We had to spend a few days in Kabul in order to have the van serviced and to allow us to visit the Embassy. We found accommodation in a small bungalow, containing a room with four beds, a sink and a table, and a bathroom with a hot shower, this seemed to be such luxury at only four pounds per night. Outside a squad of labourers was constructing a swimming pool, better we hoped than the one at Hotel Farahrod.

We headed into town to try and find advice about the border pass into Pakistan, then visited what was purported to be the 'best restaurant in town', the Bagh Bala. Although this seemed to be the eating place for Embassy Staff, who perhaps missed British cuisine, we were unimpressed by our roast beef, peas and chips. We spent an amusing afternoon in the antique shops in town, where, as Steinbeck remarked about the antique shops in Vermont, there were more antiques than could ever have been in use. Surprisingly, there seemed to be a flourishing trade in rifles, powder kegs, oil lamps and swords.

Next day we headed towards the Khyber Pass along a deep gorge about 2,000ft. deep with a blue torrent surging along the gully between tortuous jagged rock buttresses. We could just catch glimpses of white mountains in the north, possibly the Hindu Kush. We missed Customs, so Dave and Jim ate a Vesta curry, and Fred and I were invited to share a *pulau* feast with the three hospitable Customs men. A white cloth was laid on the floor and a servant carried in two steaming mounds of saffron rice, then little plates of vegetables and a plate of meat, plus four naan breads. They kindly brought two plates with a spoon and fork for us, but we managed to eat our food with our fingers, though the grains of rice round our plates showed we needed to practice. After our meal a servant appeared and poured water from a jug into a basin and we washed our hands in the running stream. Then I cleaned two sores on one man's feet and we gave them some paracetamol. He then told us, after we enquired, that the red fingernails we had seen in Afghanistan resulted from taking opium. He added that although most women we saw wore the *burka,* he himself had been to school with girls, and as they danced and mixed fairly freely here, he intended to choose his own wife.

We crossed into Pakistan through the Khyber Pass, which despite its historical significance, was a disappointment. I think I expected something more dramatic, possibly bandits and guns, rather than the men sitting around with rifles and bandoliers and the forts which topped each hill.

On our arrival in Peshawar we realised we were in a very different land. Here the roads seemed intended for traffic of all kinds and teemed with people, carts, animals and bicycles, the traffic dodging round the animals. Water buffalo, ponderous and stable, plodded their way down the main street surrounded by water pipes and bricks and swaying trucks, brightly coloured and decorated with silver and tassels. We saw corkscrew horned goats, Brahman cows, and fat tailed sheep at the edge of town, and then two trees about sixty feet high completely covered in red bougainvillea. What an assault on the senses after Afghanistan!

Lahore was amazing; we could hardly move through the streets for cows, camels, sheep, hand drawn carts, bicycle rickshaws and taxis. A herd of water buffalo wandered past with all the time in the world, while the traffic screeched and hooted and roared round them. There seemed to be beggars and men with hookahs everywhere. I drove right through the centre, nearly knocking down a traffic policeman on a stool. I stopped to take a picture and was immediately surrounded by about twenty men…a ghastly experience, never to be repeated.

That night we camped on a piece of flat deserted land by the road and ate another Vesta curry. At 9 p.m. we were about to turn in, with as usual, two in the van and two outside on the ground, when a car drove up, and four men emerged, one of them claiming to be Chairman of the Local Government of Kasur, the town next to the frontier. It was obvious that they had been on a night out and we were to be their further entertainment, we felt very vulnerable in the dark trapped inside our sleeping bags. Their spokesman said that as we were camped in a, "wild and deserted place" and were "endangered by the wild beasts of the jungle", it was his duty to "protect us in his country". We had no alternative but to follow them back to his office. There we were ushered inside where we were offered fried eggs and subjected to insolent questions. Dave's beard aroused curiosity – why did he have one – only holy people have beards – was he merely lazy? The Chairman pressed bells and forced drinks on us and the questioning turned to the, "custom of marriage in your country." In the midst of this one of his friends let out a loud b u u r p…and I nearly collapsed with giggles. At about 1 a.m. the fried eggs arrived accompanied by slices of Pakistani toast piled on a plate, and we proceeded to chase the greasy eggs with the toast. Dave

21

said he had eaten lots of toast but no egg and I broke into more giggles, whereupon I was given a spoon. After this we locked our van, and were taken to a room in the fat man's house where we sat on plastic covered chairs and were plied with orange gin and beer. Finally we were given four pillows and two blankets and we said goodnight. It was cold there sleeping fully clothed, with only a cold water urn in the courtyard for washing and an unutterably foul 'hole in the wall' for a lavatory. I was fortunate, being the only woman I was given the sofa and one rug but we missed our sleeping bags and the tent.

Next morning we were awoken by a cock crowing outside the window, some Eastern music on a radio and the clatter of a small boy running a metal hoop over the cobbles. At 8.30 a.m. one of the servants brought a delicious breakfast of vegetable curry topped with tomato and accompanied by deep fried pancakes which we tore into small pieces and wrapped round the food. Finally, after another session in the office, we were allowed to go and I found that amazingly only my treasured Voigtländer camera was missing.

We passed through Customs yet again and were now in India, again a different experience, different wildlife and new birds. The land here was very fertile and lush and there was no sign of poverty in the people or the animals, except for the dogs which were thin, one had no hair at all, very different from those in the other three countries which were huge, fluffy powerful guard dogs.

There were now ringed doves smaller than those in Scotland and fabulous green cockatoos with red beaks and long green tails which they spread out like magpies in flight. There were also huge, ugly black vultures, which looked terribly scraggy as they seemed to lose the feathers from their necks, so unkempt! On the way to Ludhiana a chipmunk flashed across the busy road in front of us. We passed water buffalo basking in water, and a blindfolded camel harnessed to a cart, walking in a circle to draw a chain of buckets raising water for irrigation. But mostly this part of the journey was like a game of dodgems – driving along the narrow raised road until we were about ten yards from an approaching bullock cart, before both we and the cart are forced down into the dusty edge.

Coming through Ludhiana we met a man who was riding an elephant. The man had a huge red canopy over his head and waved a white plumed fan whilst a girl sat on the beast's neck and controlled it with a large metal hook.

Turning into the Kulu Valley and approaching Raison, where we were to be based whilst preparing to climb our mountain, we drove up a narrow road above the Beas River which had Tibetan families engaged in road work all along its length. Road mending is the one occupation easily available to the Tibetans as it doesn't interest the locals who are farming their small plots of land. Some of the women wore beautiful long necklaces and earrings made simply out of lumps of turquoise and other stones. They shouted and waved as we passed. The weather was less welcoming, we drove through thunder and lightning and the valley was covered in grey cloud, so we couldn't yet see the Himalayas,

This verdant valley is terraced both on the valley floor and steep hillsides where, already, by 1 May, swathes of young green grain are already three feet high, down on the plains the grain has been harvested already. Fruit trees are everywhere – cherries, peaches and apricots are grown in the valley. Our host Jimmy Johnson, mainly grows Red Delicious apples which appeal more to the Indian palate than do our Pippins.

We were installed in a hut with two main rooms, and two side rooms and collected our water from a spring up the road. One room of the hut was spread with the contents of the van, pegs, ice axes, crampons, slings, ropes and carabiners, all the paraphernalia brought 7,100 miles from Benmore to achieve our dream.

We went for a wander up the road and saw a host of birds, including a dipper with a red tail behaving just like our Scottish friend, dipping up and down at the edge of the river. While we were out we happened upon a marriage dance. The bridegroom, his face hidden by a veil of gold strips and wearing a garland of rupee notes around his neck, was seated in a high chair beneath a red canopy and was carried along in a procession. The marriage procession was led by a band of drums, huge horns and a flute, which preceded about a dozen gaily dressed dancers. They formed a circle and whilst they danced two of the men waved swords around them. This ceremony would go on for three days, first at the bride's home, then at his home and presumably after that they are married.

Now at last we were getting into the real business of our expedition. We drove up to Manali and met Gan, a friend of Jimmy Johnson,

M.A. cooking outside Transit in Turkey

and he took us to see Wangyal, the Ladaki most sought after in the valley. Much to our delight, although we had been told he was unavailable, Wangyal agreed to accompany us, he arranged our porters and found another Ladaki, Zangbo, who was to cook our meals. At a fee of 15 rupees for Wangyal and 10 for Zangbo, we have both for the

Making Headlines 1969

equivalent of 22 shillings (£1.10) a day. We then went to visit members of an Anglo Indian Expedition and discovered that they had had to pay £800 on bond to the Indian Customs to cover imported food and gear. We were glad we had driven all ours out ourselves.

On our return to our camp we passed lots of sheep, curly horned goats, and ponies and foals. Outside many of the houses looms were set up with brilliant coloured wools.

Next day Wangyal came down and weighed the sacks into the 56lb loads the porters were to carry along with their own gear and food. These porters would only accompany us for three to four days up to Lower Base Camp before returning. We went to Kulu Town for last minute food, and Wangyal bought flour to make chapattis, the flat dough bread eaten widely in India. The day before our departure for the mountain, Ali Ratni Tibba, was spent in packing and writing letters. We had travelled for 7,100 fascinating and exciting miles and were prepared for the daunting challenge ahead. There were no concessions and I had to carry my small pack on top of my big one.

The First Ascent of Ali Ratni Tibba

At last, here we were now, after travelling for seven thousand miles, preparing for our first ascent of an unclimbed peak in the north of India, the Kulu Himalaya.

The giant mountain towered above me, a great peak of whiteness, which soared up into the blueness of the sky over the Himalayan range. The sun shone brightly, bathing the mountain in light, glinting on the side that was flat, plastered in snow, and absolutely vertical.

It had taken us three days to establish our base camp at 11,000ft and involved a 25-mile trek up Malana Nulla valley each carrying over 50lb. I recall that I had a small sack piled on top of my main one, and whilst trekking along a narrow ledge above a river a protruding rock knocked me off balance and into a tree. Fortunately, a branch arrested my fall, and the lads hauled me back onto the path. A mile before we reached camp, the scene became essentially black and white, devoid of green since there were shrubs and rhododendron bushes but no grass.

Our team at Base Camp, Ali Ratni is the sharp peak

Our 25 porters did not wear shoes, just straw flip-flops, and when we continued up over snow to where we wished to establish camp, they all sat down. Impasse. However, we had the money so they carried the loads the further distance and we paid them off.

With our three small tents we established base camp, with Wangyal our Sirdar, and Zangbo making their home on the snow with the food stores under a tarpaulin held up by poles. I still feel uncomfortable when I think of that but they were so cheery and did not seem to mind at all. This being before the days of Thermarests, our tiny tents were not that luxurious either but we did have foam mats, which helped to insulate us from the snow we slept on. Wangyal cooked on paraffin fired Optimus stoves, and we would sit around on sacks or upturned jerry cans, or retire to our tents, to eat our food. As time went on we got so tired of Weetabix for breakfast that for a change we had *dahl* (lentils) and rice.

It had been our intention to establish an advanced base camp, in order to put stores there to enable us to make our summit attempt from higher up, but this was not to be. Firstly we had to endure eight difficult days of continuous snow storm during which we were cramped in our tiny tents. The boys, Dave, Chris and Jim, were crammed in a small two man Arctic Guinea tent playing very lewd Scrabble and laughing outrageously. I longed to join them,

M.A. outside tent

but Fred slept on and was not keen that I should join the ribald team. I was stuck in my tent playing patience on my sleeping bag, reading and writing my diary. It was difficult as the tents became very claustrophobic and it was not possible to sit upright in case one's head touched the roof and caused a leak. Of course we had to put our boots on for the inevitable tramp out through the snow after endless cups of tea. I even washed my hair in a stream of melted glacier water so cold that I had a headache for ages.

Finally it stopped snowing and we eyed all the new whiteness and the glistening ice that plastered the rock walls. The sun would have to melt this armour from the rock before we could attempt to climb it. We dried our damp sleeping bags and gear in the sun and began to haul the loads up to Advanced Base at 13,500ft.

Prophetically I noted in my diary, *"M.A. cooked Vesta curry and tea. Beautiful area and wonderful to be yet more isolated. We are now four days march from the Kulu Valley. It could be serious in case of accident – a stretcher carry out would take about 10 days"*.

The very next day disaster struck. Early in the morning Jim, Chris and Dave set off to explore higher up. The snow at that time of day was brick hard because it had been freezing all night, and theoretically it was the safest time to cross the glaciers. Suddenly we heard shouts. They became louder. "Rope, rope". Fred and I looked up the slope and instead of three figures there were only

M.A. breaking trail

two. Jim had fallen 80ft into a crevasse. The opening had been hidden under a layer of deep snow. Wangyal took up a rope, and with Jim cutting steps inside the walls of the crevasse with his axe, we got him out. I shuddered when I looked down into the crevasse as it must have been over 200ft deep. Blue green ice beckoned. With gentle poking we ascertained that Jim had two cracked ribs, but his back was OK. We gave him painkillers and sweet tea and strapped him up, so that he could lean against a pile of ropes and packs and jackets, to try and ease the discomfort.

Of course this shed a completely new light on our trip. After travelling for seven thousand miles, the whole expedition was suddenly now pitched on the point of painful uncertainty and doubt. For two days we agonised about what to do. But we all felt that Jim was the most important factor. We examined our consciences and spent a day doing a practice climb and thinking it over. Then one night we were awoken by Jim calling out in pain. He had rolled over on his sleeping mat onto his cracked ribs. Fred and I decided he had to go out…so we started down with Jim bravely walking slowly on the snow, and Wangyal and Zangbo carrying his gear. He walked so well that he persuaded us to go back up and try the mountain the next day with Chris and Dave. We were now off the deep snow and the going would be easier for him as he descended on to grass. We agreed somewhat reluctantly for we shared Jim's deep disappointment and brave attitude.

It had been a tiring day and I noted in my diary, *"back up the glacier to Advanced Base, arriving supperless at 8 p.m. No time for supper, a tin of fish and tea, then packed up gear to go on the mountain first light – 3 a.m."*.

I took a light sleeping pill in the hope I would get a little sleep…we had four hours in bed. A silly idea, as I was in a complete daze at 3 a.m. At 3.30, after Weetabix and tea, we were off across crisp, hard snow to the foot of the ramp where we roped up. I stumbled about in a sleepy fog. We were all wearing crampons. The spikes bit into the snow and we felt secure and positive, yet there was apprehension about what lay ahead. We zigzagged up the steep slope and felt very nervous as, plunging the shafts of our ice axes deep into the snow, we crossed a slope which by day, for 100 yards, is swept by avalanches. This still being night the snow was frozen solid and would remain so until the sun hit it later.

We made it to a col, and then took off our crampons, for we were now to climb on rock. My diary again: *"To begin with the climbing was quite difficult with steep rock slabs, and thin cracks…then became more broken with rock chimneys."* At 17,000ft I began to move more slowly, with frequent stops, and developed a splitting headache due to altitude sickness. Dave brewed up some melted sweeties on our Camping Gaz stove and gave me some heavy-duty painkillers as we had nothing less. So that, rattling from all these pills, sleeping pills and now strong painkillers, I proceeded uphill, still with a headache and dozing off on belays.

As we were not going to make the summit that day, we decided to bivouac and found a large flat piece of snow surrounded by large granite blocks, so that we did not have to be fixed by pegs to the site. Often when bivouacking, or sleeping on a ledge, to keep one from falling off, one ties oneself to the rope and then fixes the rope by metal pegs or by slinging it round a rock spike. I cooked up some dehydrated food, but the rice tasted like pebbles, no one wanted any so we had some tea before trying to sleep. The ledge on which we spent the night

M.A. cooking on bivouac

had a sheer drop of 4,000ft on one side, it was not long enough to stretch out on and I lay with my head resting on a granite outcrop. In the middle of the night I struggled out of my sleeping bag and put on boots to go to the edge of the ledge to have a cautious pee without falling 4,000ft. On the way back I dropped one boot. To my horror, it was not mine, it was Fred's. Potentially this was very, very serious, no boot on snow at that height would probably have resulted in frostbite for that foot. I hardly dared to confess to what I had done, but I had to. We were so lucky, the boot had lodged on a ledge eight feet below.

Breakfast consisted of muesli with tepid melted snow water and powdered milk. I felt that I would just like to stay on the ledge, but finally having little alternative, I forced myself to follow upwards. We reached the summit at 10 a.m. after two hours of staggeringly slow progress. Finally on a snow slope with some large rocks, we saw we could go no higher. Terrific feeling. The summit was a rock ridge and as Dave joked, "Ladies first!" I went on up, and sure enough. "This IS the summit," I yelled. Amazing feeling, I was the first person ever to set foot on the peak of Ali Ratni Tibba.

Dave, M.A. and Fred on summit of Ali Ratni Tibba

We had to go down. After hammering a horseshoe into a crack we started our abseils down the rope to the col. Nine rope lengths. We then had to cross a glacier in the afternoon when the snow is soft and you sink in so far. I had developed a poisoned heel, to compensate for the headache, which had now gone, and could not pull my foot out, so had to wait for one of the boys to pull it out. To make it worse, my boot would sink through the crust and embed itself in the snow below so that I was skinning my knees on frozen crust. Fred had gone on ahead, ashamed of me, I think. We made it, and Wangyal welcomed us back with soup and endless mugs of tea. We were too tired and not hungry, our lack of appetite not being helped by thought of more lentils or yet another Vesta curry.

After a disturbed but relieved night in a warm sleeping bag in a tent, I examined my purple and swollen ankle and decided I had to lance it. Taking my Swiss Army Knife and opening the big blade, I took a deep breath and pushed the tip of the blade into my skin. Gratifyingly it produced a large amount of poison, so I felt justified in having found it impossible to walk the previous day. I dosed it with antibiotic powder and took some penicillin, but then found I could not get my boot on. I sat there on an old sack wearing flip-flops and feeling worn out, worried and a bit lost. But next day I found that by wearing a double boot as a single I could hobble, so we got down to base camp where the snow had disappeared and the flowers were sprinkling the old yellowed grass with colour.

After summit,
a cup of tea

We spent a night at Malana village, where Wangyal and Zangbo cooked us chapattis, which we ate with a tin of butter and apricot jam that Jim had sent back up. We ate too much not having had any fats since Turkey, so we all had to lie down flat to recover. We shared a room in the Headman's house with women who were sitting on the mud floor whilst suckling their children. A man beat a drum and whilst the women wailed a Hindu song, another man danced round the fire on the floor. A wonderful night, after which we slept hardly a wink as squeaking mice cavorted across our sleeping bags and over our heads.

Carrying a big stick, as there were bears there, we made it to the valley, bushwhacking through the birch and carpets of wild flowers that had appeared when the snow melted. There we met up with Jim, brown and cheerful, having been lavishly entertained by Jimmy Johnson, the wealthy orchard owner, who offered us wonderful, fresh, sweet black cherries from his trees.

Dave had already gone to Delhi to fly home, so the four of us finally drove down the Kulu Valley and made our own way to Delhi. We spent a few days there and bought some fabulous raw silk in the Cottage Industries shop. Jim was staying at the Youth Hostel, but Fred and I were in a hotel where, for two pounds a night, we luxuriated in air conditioning and sheets. Chris arranged for us to travel first class on the train to Agra. This gave us breakfast of tea in a china cup, two hard-boiled eggs and three potato chips on the side of a greasy plate, and toast. And so we visited the famous Taj Mahal, busy with tourists but even so an enjoyable experience.

We then went on to Fatehpur Sikri, an abandoned town founded in 1569 by Akbar the Mughal Emperor and which served as the capital of his empire until 1585 when it was relocated to Fatehabad. Here the huge red sandstone palace once housed 1,000 concubines, 2,000 horses, 4,000 camels and elephants.

After this it was time to head home. So we retraced our journey out but this time also had the company of a Danish ex-Hippie whom Jim had found in the Youth Hostel. He paid us $70 to take him back. I suffered from appalling gut problems for days on the way back and can only remember lying in the hot furnace of the Transit van wishing for it all to be over.

We ended up by climbing in the Calanques in the South of France on the way home, and the van was broken into. After journeying 15,000 miles, to be robbed at this point seemed ridiculous.

We made it back home and were glad to be back in Scotland where we found that the papers were full of our ascent:

'SCOTS CLIMBERS conquer peak in Himalayas'
(*Glasgow Herald*)

CHAPTER THREE

Climbs

To The Bugaboos, 1985

Crowded in the corner of the pub in Aviemore, recovering from the latest Ski Instructor Course on Cairngorm, spirits were high; relief. It's a very stressful fortnight where pressure is tough. You could be failed for wearing the wrong jacket! If it's out of date.

A group of friends and new friends. Chat turns happily to other things. Andy is going to sea kayak across to Rum this week. He suddenly says: "I am going to climb in the Bugaboos this summer, but have no one to climb with".

I said, without blinking, "I'll come" I had not met Andy before but he seemed cheery and positive and it sounded too good a chance to miss. I had seen photographs of these marvellous rock towers at the Lodge. I wanted to go.

The seed was sown, and nurtured. A few preliminary checkups with mutual friends…is Andy ok? Is he a good safe climber? Etc…and I booked my flight to Vancouver.

'The Bugaboos' lie in eastern British Columbia, a mountain range in the Purcell Mountains. Originally named the Nunataks, until a mining expedition in the late 1800s near Bugaboo Falls caused them to be renamed. They are actually monster Nunataks, easily visible when you fly over them to Vancouver from the east. (A nunatak is defined as a small point of rock emerging above ice sheets or glaciers predominently in the Arctic and Antarctic, but also in other glaciated regions. In Scotland two prominent Nunataks are Suilven and Stac Pollaidh). These nunataks are very large granite spires.

"M.A. what are you doing between my legs?"

"I'm terrified."

We are sitting on top of Bugaboo Spire. I had seen the ominous dark clouds of the storm approaching up the valley below us, and here we were. Lightning flashed and the rock crackled.

33

"Time to be out of here," shouted Andy as he prepared to abseil down the side of the granite spire. He was gone. It was not a good spot to be alone. Lightning whizzed past me, so that I thought a plane was going past, and I said to myself, don't be silly, it's not a plane, it's lightning. I am wrapped in thick mist. I grab the rope when it comes slack, as I know Andy is off the rope and standing on a ledge, then I attach my karabiner to the rope and start off down. More whizzing and more thunder, and the rope wringing wet. A perfect lightning conductor. It's lashing rain.

We make it down, and find a chipmunk has eaten a hole in our food bag and enjoyed some rice and nuts. I reflect on where I have brought myself. Carrying 80lbs (30kg) of food and gear up 2,000ft to the hut two days previously, up steel ladders, with no sight of Andy who scampered off ahead. I remember feeling my knees lock under the weight!

Undaunted by the storm, a new day saw us off to climb the southwest ridge of Pigeon Spire, rising up out of the glacier. Half way up the ridge I saw a couple following up. I thought I recognised the voice. "Mhairi is that you? This is M.A."

Well. This girl I had last seen at Glenmore Lodge in Scotland ten years ago where she was our domestic bursar. She had married a well-known Glasgow rock climber, Davy Todd, and there they were, on Pigeon!

We waited for them, then of course there were hugs and exclamations, but we had to finish our climbs! Then we all descended, and I have not seen them since!

It snowed heavily, so all plans of further climbs were abandoned and we descended to the roadhead. We decided to head for Banff and think again. Andy got a lift in a pickup with our gear, and I just said, "Don't worry about me, I'll be fine, I'll hitch and join you at the Youth Hostel in Banff".

I do this sort of thing all the time…jump in and then think! It was not easy. I sat at the side of the Trans-Canada Highway watching massive motorhomes trundle past, with two passengers sitting three feet apart in their posh seats, and me, sitting leaning against a tree reading Ian Hibbell's book *'Into Remote Places'*. How apt. My luck changed and a VW Camper drove into the parking lot, a young lad wound the window down and said, "where you headed? Banff? Climb in".

I climbed in and we chatted away, and he pulled out a loaf of bread he had baked that day and gave it to me. We found Andy at the Youth Hostel, and I waved the lad goodbye.

A new adventure awaited us as we took over as short-term wardens of the hut on Mount Victoria.

Bugaboo Spire

Andy and M.A.

Climbing Toubkal in Morocco solo, 1988

Nieve Penitente

Marrakesh Airport, the palm tree fronds waved against the dying red of the sunset sky. The last bus had departed with the tourists off the plane and I found myself with only a rucksack, alone and in the dark, apart from two taxi drivers who were wearing *djellabas* and talking in Arabic.

I deliberated, it was dark and I could not walk into town. I had booked a room at the Hotel Ifni, where my friend Hamish Brown had often stayed during the many years he roamed the Atlas Mountains. He was to be my talisman on my own wanderings amongst the Berbers, as he had a huge depth of knowledge of the terrain and people of the mountains of Morocco. Eventually I approached the taxi drivers; one wanted the lift but not the rucksack, the other would take the rucksack but would charge a lot extra. Then as I waivered a fight ensued and my pack ended up locked in the boot of the 'other' man's taxi. I had no choice but to follow my rucksack – very scary in the dark and under-standing nothing of the Arabic being spoken.

When we got to Marrakesh I went into the hotel, which was on the famous Djemma el Fna, a lively open market where all the acrobats perform. I did not understand what was going on but was told to get

36

into a car and then was driven off through the night. I had no idea where I was going but eventually arrived in a compound, with a large house and a lot of children. It transpired that this house belonged to the owner of the hotel and, as there had been no room for me there, I was to spend the night as their guest. It was not an auspicious start, though I had made it perfectly clear that Hamish, who was regarded as Mr Morocco by the local mountain people, was my friend and, I felt, my talisman. He had been coming to Morocco for a very long time and had completed many interesting treks there. Trustingly, I felt that no one would harm me if I was Hamish's friend!

The *Sunday Times* had reported on a fatality on the Tazaghart plateau near Toubkal in 1987, where a young man, part of a Sherpa 'trekking holiday', had slipped and disappeared off the edge of a snow slope onto rocks below. I wanted to find out for myself what the situation was. I was leading for Sherpa but would not have undertaken to lead on something so serious and of a mountaineering nature.

There also had been another fatality for another company and I intended to go and have a look at it myself. I did feel quite anxious as a woman alone in the mountains of Morocco, which is not at all the same as being in the Alps in Europe. One does not know 'the rules' and there are few walkers around. In the mountains I was able to speak French with the Berbers and others – *"Je suis amie de Hamish!"*

Staying in a small hut in Imlil, I met up with some French people and they invited me to join them for a short side trip. Then I made it to the Neltner Hut (10,498ft) with the idea of climbing Toubkal (13,671ft) in the Atlas Mountains, the highest mountain in North Africa. The hut was old, cold and grotty with dirty blankets and a rather swarthy warden. (In 1999 it was a Club Alpin Francais hut, but has since been replaced by the smart Refuge des Mouflons) I was up at five, and making my coffee in the basement, which passed as a kitchen, when I met two French guys also intent on climbing Toubkal. As in similar situations, I wanted to do this one alone, without companions, therein lies the challenge and the satisfaction.

I left on my own out of the back of the hut and ascended the scree behind the hut. This is much easier if there is some snow cover, otherwise it's a case of one step forward and two back. As it was June, there was still some hard snow, and my crampons held firm and it was not

M.A. in Ikhibi Sud of Toubkal

Toubkal Summit

difficult. Then it was time to traverse a hanging valley, the Ikhibi Sud, there was no sign of the French climbers and I rejoiced in having the place to myself. The Ikhibi Sud is covered by a floor of strange spikey snow ridges, called *nieve penitente*. These are tall thin blades of snow or ice that tend to lean towards the sun so that they resemble penitents doing penance. Darwin first experienced them in 1839 when walking from Santiago de Chile to Mendoza. I straddled the formations in my crampons. Crunch, crunch. It would have been difficult had I lost my balance here, and it was awkward using my ice axe, a climbing rather than a walking axe, for support because it was too short to reach the snow. I just had to balance.

On the top I met the two French guys and we took one another's photographs. I am not sure, but they must have taken a slightly different route, although I was on the *'Voie normale'*. I ate a hard-boiled egg, slurped down some water, and munched a biscuit whilst enjoying the excellent view. There was no one else up there. Now, Hamish tells me, the summit often has 200 people on it and the two huts barely provide enough accommodation for the people. How different it all is after 20 years. This reminds me of climbing Mt Blanc in 1968 when we were the only people on the top. Now, as you can see from far off with binoculars, it is black with people.

I loved Morocco and did return many times as a leader with Sherpa Expeditions, but mostly went to the Jebel Sahro in the south, or to the Mgoun.

Afterword: As Toubkal is so easy of access...fly into Marrakech, 1,529ft, then take a bus and taxi to Asni and Imlil. It can be possible to 'do' Toubkal in a few days, but as the CAF Hut is at nearly 10,500ft one should beware that altitude sickness can strike fast if one has flown in from the UK four days ago. I had actually met French folk in Imlil and gone with them to the Tazaghat Refuge over the Tizi n'Tzikert for one night, then I had had a hairy solo traverse over the hills and down to the Neltner Hut. But in those days of going to Nepal a lot my body was used to thin air!

The Sahro

Laden mule

Angus and Mule

Trekking and Climbing on Mount Kenya, 1994

View of Mt Kenya, Nelion and Batian

'Jambo, abari?' (Hello, how are you?) Our porter, Boniface, met us as we tumbled out of our jeep at Chogoria. We had driven up from Nairobi at 110kph as our driver put his foot down and we tore through villages scattering hens, children, and ladies in vibrant coloured skirts carrying baskets on their heads. Dust flew as huts behind stockades, where goats and cows snoozed in the heat, groves of coffee, tea and maize sped past. Large trees were draped with purple bougainvillea, and acacia and jacaranda and palms lined the road. New birds, a giant egret and a crowned crane flew by, then a truck with fish hanging off the wing mirror passed us.

I had planned to try to climb Mount Kenya and Kilimanjaro in January 1994, but my mother had died on 31 December and this hit me hard. I no longer felt I wanted to peel myself off familiar soil and go to Africa. I had smashed my toe on a table leg in the kitchen and rather hoped it might be broken so that I could not go, but it was not. So I flew out, with Rob Collister my friend and guide, and his friend Chris.

We planned to walk in to Mount Kenya from Chogoria on the east side, and having then climbed it, we hoped we would walk out to the

Naro Moru side on the west, and return to Nairobi. From there we would head off to Tanzania and climb Kilimanjaro.

I had bought *'Collins Guide to Birds of East Africa'* in Nairobi, and spent happy times at the end of each day, identifying all the wonderfully exotic new birds such as weaver birds which enter their hanging nests through a hole at the bottom.

My diary records: *"set off on a sandy track, giant heather, Helichrysum (everlasting flowers), and blue Aquiligia and it's hot and windless through the six foot high heather. Malachite sunbird flies past. Wonderful walk, thrashing through bamboo and thick vegetation to Lake Ellis, where we found a flat campsite on the north side on our own."*

This is all so new and different. I was surprised to see tents on the south side. Giant groundsel with a yellow flower and giant lobelia, three feet high, down by the lakeside. We walked through huge tussock grass interspersed with cabbage groundsel and occasionally with open meadows.

We sat with the porters at their fire and learnt that they are Meru men, and all Protestants who had been baptised and given English names by the Church of Scotland Mission, which came out in the 1930s.

Camp by Lake Michelson

So we had Wycliffe, Phineas, Lloyfor and Boniface. Boniface was memorable as he had a coal black face and wore a white hat fashioned from an old white football, cut to fit. Wycliffe had a BA in Sociology but earned more as a porter or leader, and said the government want to send him to be an agricultural officer, but he *"not must"* go.

As the smoke rose in the cold night we snacked on charred maize and coffee, brewed in an old pot on the hot red embers. A tall groundsel was silhouetted behind us against a fading sky. Voices murmured and sleep and a warm bag beckoned.

The next morning was beautiful; shafts of golden light lit up the hill on the other side of the lake, with flashes of red from the tents nestled below. A hyrax was sunning himself on a rock. There was a thick frost on the inside of my flysheet and my breath left visible, temporary clouds in the air. The flysheet crackled as I brushed it and the frost crystals landed on my sleeping bag. I smoothed them off and extracted the gas cylinder from inside my sleeping bag to make a brew for Chris and Rob. (If I had not kept it warm it would not have given me gas for ages.)

We took our time walking in, as to ascend too fast would mean not acclimatising and the possibility of succumbing to potentially dangerous altitude sickness. Chogoria was at 10,000ft and Lake Michaelson at 12,998ft so we were already high and noticed the altitude affecting us on ascents. It was hard work, we were short of breath.

We were aiming for Lake Michaelson below and Rob and I took the shorter route, clambering over tussocks and falling down stone chutes, and arriving 20 minutes after everyone else. We put up our tents and in no time mountain chats arrived, also a mouse, which retreated with a whole digestive biscuit, bigger than itself, stolen from my tent. A rock hyrax tried his luck with the packet of peas but scurried off when Rob threw a boot at him. The hyrax are like large guinea pigs and give a warning whistle like a marmot. That night I took out my binoculars and we let the Meru guys look at the moon and the stars. This led to them asking us to explain what an atomic bomb is, but Rob and I failed at the starting gate of splitting atoms etc.

Time to try climbing. I offered to carry a rope as we went off to climb 'The Hat'. Hard to remember about gear; Sticht plate, harness, hat, slings. This was not just a fun walk across the Kenya highlands!

As we clambered, heaving and puffing, past huge tree groundsel, I wondered if trying to climb Mount Kenya was a good idea. I do get sold on ideas! Good friction on the rock and then after we were on the summit, Rob lowered me down, which I do not like, but better get used to it.

I passed a terrible night, possibly due to a premonition or fear of what is ahead. In the long lonely hours I read *'Evil Cradling'* Brian Keenan's story of four and a half years as a hostage in Beirut, and listened to Paul Simon.

But it was wonderful waking to the sound of mountain chats' flapping wings outside the tent, and a hyrax scuffling around in the grass. These times are so special, lying quietly in a tent, listening to birds' wings flapping, when normally one never hears them. We create our own noise so much. When I looked out there were eight hyrax, some eating tangerine peel attracted by the pungent smell. The boys had the fire going and sitting down on a stone, I joined them for a mug of coffee.

American Camp named after Yvon Choinard and an American, Mike Covington, who came here to straighten out the route in the Diamond Couloir, lies at 14,353ft. There was a group here filming the inspiring story narrated by Felice Benuzzi in his book *'No Picnic on Mount Kenya'*. This is about three Italian Prisoners of War who, in 1943, led by Benuzzi, gazed at Mount Kenya from their British POW camp, and decided to escape and try to climb it. They had saved their rations and made do with gear they made up secretly in camp. The only route map they had was the map off an Oxo tin in camp. After three of them escaped out of the camp, one got sick, so two of them headed out on their own. They had no guidebook and did not quite make the summits of Batian or Nelion. When they came down they handed themselves in at the camp and were given 28 days of solitary confinement, reduced to seven days as the commandant applauded their 'sporting effort'.

At 17,057ft, Mount Kenya is the second highest mountain in Africa, only Kilimanjaro is higher at 19,340ft. The guidebook says, "You need to be a technical mountaineer, armed with ropes and a full harness of climbing gear". The trekkers' summit is Point Lenana, which nowadays is straightforward, though it used to have snow and ice on it and required crampons. Mount Kenya has two summits, Nelion and Batian, which is 36ft higher. Fifteen years ago I had seen photographs of the Diamond Glacier, which hung between Nelion and Batian in the Gate of the Mists, and this had fired my imagination to go there. That glacier no longer exists. It has melted. The landscape was all and more than I had ever anticipated from seeing slides twenty years previously. There are high snowy peaks reaching up to a blue sky, where cumulus clouds frequently hug the tops. Mount Kenya is all rock, a mixture in which syenite, a form of granite, predominates. It stands out very black against the snowy mountains, surrounded by green slopes and ravines. Below glistens Lake Michaelson, but all around is the strange vegetation of groundsels and lobelias.

We have to cross the Lewis Glacier to get to the start of the climb. We did another practice climb, on Midget Peak. *"Very windy, I feel absolutely buggered. Six pitches up a gully where Shipton and Tilman reportedly had an epic in the 1930s. Chris and I climbed together until we had to rope up and climb fearsome holdless corners with, fortunately, excellent friction. Last two pitches wild, then balancing on a ridge, with nothing either side but a drop hundreds of feet down. Very fearsome. Rob lowered me off twenty feet on an Italian hitch, I hate this."*

The rest of the descent was in hail, through rocks and groundsel and tussocks. I experienced fear, apprehension, exhaustion, elation and finally a feeling of satisfaction for doing it at all. That night we were told there were leopards about, so I was scared to go out to pee. I was told they prefer hyrax!

We had intended to climb Point John but the film crew had bagged it. Not content with the superb epic nature of the real story they had concocted a 'love interest' where the men had a duel for the hand of a lady, taking place on a Tyrolean traverse high on Point John. (A Tyrolean Traverse is a method of crossing space between two points on a horizontal rope). Chatting to them, Rob found that he knew some of the climbing crew. Rick Ridgeway, a well-known American climber was in charge of the filming/climbing team. He was very taken with Boniface's hat and wanted it in the film. As Boniface refused to sell it a porter was dispatched to the nearest market town to find a white football to make a replica!

44

Instead of Point John we climbed Point Lenana at 16,635ft considered to be the third peak of Mount Kenya and often climbed by trekking groups.

We packed for the Big Climb. I washed my hair and some smelly clothes in the morning, then we set off for Top Hut. Wycliffe carried the climbing gear and food, and I staggered up with my own gear and suffered an attack of urgent runs, so dived behind a cabbage groundsel – my nerves again.

We meet some Army guys at the Austrian Hut, who are going to climb Batian, "Nelion's a hard climb. You OK with that?" all I need. I ask him if he is Scottish he sounds it…"Och aye!" he confirms.

Mountain House slop again, eaten out of the bag. Rob and I climb aloft onto the sleeping shelf, while Chris finishes his book downstairs. No sleep but when it did come a door banged and I shot up out of my bed, "Where am I?" The Army guys had left the door ajar. Rob closed it. Coffee, muesli and yesterday's jammy dry rolls at 5 a.m., and we left.

We crossed the Lewis Glacier, I in my gym shoes, as my toe has not healed enough to walk in boots, though I will manage to climb. I hope.

"Rob I must stop, I'm blowing up with heat."

"Make it quick." We are roped, so if I stop we all stop. Climbing is always like this in the mountains. I remember in Chamonix one seemed to be going up as fast as possible, so as to be up and down again before the weather broke.

Chris arrived at the foot of the rock, he was wrecked. Rob was impatient to start. We do, and overtake the Army lads very soon. Moving together, Chris and I ten feet apart, Rob ahead. I was out of breath but somehow kept going.

Climbing Nelion (Rob Collister)

Climbing was good, and I found I was enjoying it, past Baillie's Bivvy. (Rusty Bailie had spent years climbing in and around Mount Kenya and was credited with putting up this old bivvy hut on the route. He is, and was, a very well-known mountaineer and was from South Africa. He came to work as Fred's deputy at Glenmore Lodge)

Looking over at Diamond Couloir, and Batian, up and up and it's the top. Howell's Bivvy and what a feeling. We are on Nelion (17,020ft) and across the gap is Batian (17,0757ft). Three and a half hours. For once I 'enjoyed the journey' which is unusual for me on a long climb. We lay around for an hour on the top in the sun, extraordinary views for Mount Kenya stands apart from everywhere. We could see the film crew on Point John, still on some pinnacle.

The Army guys came and departed for Batian, 140m away across the Gate of the Mists, but we decided enough was enough. We decided another five or six hours easily to descend to the Gate of the Mists, ascend Batian, and then reverse it all. The guidebook even recommends two days for the two summits.

Down and down. Lowered and abseiling. Changed out of my boots into my gym shoes. Then slithering on the soft snow of the glacier. "Come on M.A., it's OK," said Rob as he trotted down the smooth polished rock of the Lewis Glacier. I dried my gym shoe soles on my trouser legs by running my feet down the cloth, and followed.

Tired. Crotchety, headache, cold and the runs. After a meal of pasta and vegetables, which I didn't want, I collapsed in my tent at 7.30. *"Slept and snored till dawn, 6 a.m. Heard leopard or something snuffling outside my tent, lost a sock"*.

Next day we were off at 8 a.m. Funny anti-climactic feeling and not terribly looking forward to Kilimanjaro and more *Sturm and Drang*. We stopped for our lunch at an idyllic spot surrounded by rocks covered in yellow saxifrage.

Then Rob said, "I may not be going to Kili, I feel I have a chest infection, and friends of mine died on Everest when going high like this". He also thought we might catch it. Awful discussion. Rob said he might go home early, but would arrange for us to have a guide on Kili. Chris said he would go home too. I had taken my savings out to come to Africa and after waiting 15 years to get here I was not prepared to give all this up. We continued on down in silence.

A short way down the path, Rob has stopped and says he is very upset. I am in tears. We talk it through and hug one another and say we will have a good time, doing something else. He is a great person, and it had hurt me so much that we had upset one another. But I felt that knowing him, on this occasion, I had to say what I thought and not acquiesce and keep quiet.

We descend the Vertical Bog (what? it's dry!) and drive to meet our agent. No one has booked us in at Naro Moru. Several hours, Fantas and cold chips later, we are minibus-bound for Nairobi. Chris is pointing out bee-eaters, kites, pied crows, and Marabou storks. I'm looking at bananas, passion fruit terraces, maize, sisal, coffee trees and tea. Moses hears Chris coughing and me sneezing and says; "You go to Kili?" Well. Actually no. So no *Sturm and Drang*!

"Kwaheri"...goodbye to our men who will return to Chogoria. We had enjoyed their company. Boniface to his home and family, he has built his own house and grows maize, carrots, cabbage, 15 banana trees and fifty coffee trees and tends a cow, hens, and seven beehives.

We booked into our hotel, ordered beers and I found I had a palatial room with a huge double bed. We all bathed, and trampled our clothes in the hot water in the bath before having a marginal cheap supper out. And started to plan the plan to replace Kilimanjaro!

STAGE TWO

Birds and animals. We bought a mammal guide and I had my bird guide. We were off to Parks, birds and climbs. A holiday? Rob and Chris spent a lot of time organising the next week: Lake Naivasha for bird watching, and some climbing at Hell's Gate, then off to the Masai Mara to look at animals. It sounded perfect.

We hired a jeep that jolted across roads so rough that my head bumped off the roll bar. The ride to Fisherman's Camp at Lake Naivasha was tedious, bumping through potholes at 20kph, past an ostrich farm, the land grey and sandy on both sides, brown grass. Chris had opted to be the 'named driver'. When we were stopped by a policeman for 'speeding', which seemed unlikely on this road, he was given the choice of going to Nairobi and waiting a week to appear in court and be fined 600 shillings, or to; "give it to me and you can go on your way!"

Then we found Lake Naivasha, which was rather grey in the late afternoon heat and dust. But Fisherman's Camp seemed to be a staging post for trans Africa trucks. Many here. Someone said there might be hippos at night in the camp. A warning not to stray outside the Banda.

Our Banda, a little brown wooden hut, with a bamboo roofed terrace, and four bamboo chairs outside, was set back from the reeds that encircle the Lake and the huge trees soaring skywards behind us.

I pushed open the door and saw we had four beds, a shower and a loo. Great. I cooked our soup outside on a shelf, and gazed up at myriad stars in a black sky. Even the mosquitoes seemed to be asleep. I felt that I would be happy here for a week.

Six a.m., Chris sat on me in my sleeping bag, and pulled at my feet. "Get up M.A., its birdwatching time!" The fish eagle had perched himself atop the highest tree and woken everyone up. The dawn chorus started up.

For over three hours we just stood there with our binoculars, watching endless colourful birds flit past. Kingfishers and shrikes, bulbuls and sunbirds, herons and cormorants. Then there were vultures and buzzards and a huge secretary bird flew by. Little rufous sparrows pecked round the grass by the Banda. I absolutely loved this time, and we had three mornings of this. I have never forgotten them.

As day broke, we went off to Hell's Gate to climb. A wonderful route up Fischer's Tower. Well, I was so fit. We saw zebra and I said I wanted to see buffalo. We saw a whole herd at a water hole.

Then, time to move on. We met up with the safari guys at Limuru, and a mixed bag of Hungarians, Turks, and New Zealanders, and us. Candelabra trees, (Euphorbia) and Thorn trees (Acacia) here and a scorching sun. We were given lunch outside under a tree and a cat appeared that liked sausage and scratched at my legs to get it. Cats always know I am a soft touch!

After a drive of about four hours to the Masai Mara Park we found seven tatty tents, some with broken zips and damp foam mattresses, which were wet after the recent storm. We were on a cheap deal so it was fine. Two shacks served as a kitchen, one as a dining room with thin slices of wood as tables, but they managed to serve up chicken, rice, veggie curry, and pineapple. There was a bonfire outside and Rob and I talked quietly while thunder rolled and lightning flashed continuously in the dark night, and rain lashed down outside our shack. I could hear it battering the leaves of the vegetation.

We were told the toilet was behind our tent in the bushes. No way. I heard elephant bashing about in those bushes. A tall thin Masai warrior sat on a chair beside our tents with a hurricane lamp beside him. He held a long spear. Our guard.

I appear to have mislaid my sleeping bag. From my diary, I find I went to my tent and slept in T-shirt, fleece, polar long johns, trousers and socks but woke at 2 a.m., frozen. I called out to Chris and Rob and joined them in their tent, sticking my feet in Chris's sleeping bag. I warmed up.

At 6.30 next morning we were up and off. In our old VW van. Into the Park to see what was to be seen. The top was rolled back and we stood looking out over its roof. As we drove around we saw giraffes and elephants, hippos in the river, a rhino with her baby and lots of gazelles plus a small herd of wildebeest. We were out for six and a half hours, and it was fantastic. Lots of birds again.

We returned for a slap up lunch of stew, mashed potatoes, vegetables and salad, followed by mango, passion fruit and pineapple salad.

Another cold night but this time I shared with Chris, sleeping top to toe in my grotty tent. As I put on face cream Chris said, "It's not like sharing with Rob" and we both giggled.

Another early start, and this time we were to see a pride of lions; about seven lionesses and fifteen cubs of differing ages, feeding off an old buffalo carcass. The saddest thing was to see an old lion, threatened and then attacked by all the lionesses, who drove him off. His days as chief of the pack are over, he's old and injured and can no longer hunt; they want a new young male. He wandered off into the future. Alone.

Next morning after a wonderful send-off breakfast of runny eggs, sausages and toast we set off towards Limuru, and then to Nairobi. Poor Rob. I talked to him about my next dreams, the Wind Rivers, the Matterhorn. Am I flying kites?

Back in Nairobi, first off is a bath and oh what filthy water! What a great trip we have had. In a way it reminded me of the climbing trip I made to the Bugaboos in Canada with Andy in 1984. It has opened more doors. It is possible to just go out there, and DO what you want instead of just wishing you could…living the dreams.

And Rob has agreed to go to the Matterhorn with me later this year.

Climbing the Matterhorn with Rob Collister, 23 July 1994

View of Matterhorn

"Of our dreams are born the great joys of life.
But one must have dreams"

Gaston Rebuffat, Starlight and Storm

The Matterhorn rises up behind Zermatt, hiding itself from view as one travels up in the train from the valley, until leaning out of the window and craning one's neck to the right, one can catch a view of it. It is spell-binding and imposing, rising as it does alone at the end of the valley, commanding a presence all of its own. I had viewed it many times on ski holidays and when walking across on the High Level Route from Chamonix and had wondered if I would actually ever climb it. It stands at 14,692 ft, an isolated triangle at the end of the valley. It is an icon – in fact to many it does symbolise Switzerland.

The train shuddered to a halt. As people clambered down onto the platform, the porters from the local hotels trundled the high trolleys alongside the train to take the suitcases on up the main street to the hotels. The wheels rattle and judder over the rough tarmac, for no cars are allowed in Zermatt, just increasingly, electric cars belonging to the hotels, these purr past and as you don't hear them it's easy to get run over. I took myself and my rucksack across to the Bahnhof Hotel, behind the station, and booked myself in with Paula Biner, whose family had owned it for a long time. This hotel has a special place in the heart of climbers in Zermatt; Frau Biner's husband was a guide.

The whole idea had taken hold in my mind when I was at school in Switzerland in 1957. I had been introduced to climbing and our guide, Charles Louis, told us we would climb the Matterhorn in the summer at the end of term. I was one of three girls at the school who had become regular and keen rock climbers at weekends. Imagine! Unfortunately, I felt obliged to return home as my mother was excited about presenting me to the Queen at Holyrood that summer, and although it was the very last thing I wanted, I felt it right to do what she had planned. If it had not been for my mother, I would never have gone to school in Switzerland in the first place nor had the chance to ski and climb. Payback time.

So here I was...July 1994, having climbed Mt Kenya in January with Rob Collister, a mountain guide and friend from North Wales, I was all fired up to tick off another box and the idea of going for the Matterhorn this same year had entered my head. Rob told me that Nelion, on Mount Kenya was a more technical climb than the Matterhorn, though not so long. I am not sure I am into comparisons like this. Rob agreed to take me

Rob on Trifthorn

on the mountain, and we met in Zermatt. Having just taken a group of clients along the High Level Route I felt leg and altitude fit!

We decided to climb the 12,231ft Trifthorn first, as a training climb. We set off to the Rothornhutte through luscious green grass, sprinkled with gen-tians and saxifrage under a blue sky and a hot sun. I am feeling strong and good. Rob is surprised, "You must have a headache", "No," I say, "I am fine, just a bit tired." It was very hot with a huge pack. "Well if you are not feeling the altitude you must be exceptional". I am! Rob a bit silent, has he got a headache! He had forgotten that I had just done the High Level Route, walking from Chamonix to Zermatt.

Next day called for a 3.30 a.m. rise, and of course I felt as if I had not slept at all. It was wonderful to leave after bread and jam and steaming hot coffee. On with the head torch and the beam picks up loose rocks and beaten earth as we find our way in the dark. Then we are trotting over the rocks in the moonlight and across the glacier, crunching hard snow underfoot and skirting crevasses. I noted that we had a full moon on Mount Kenya too this year. Rope tight between us, we overtake a Swiss rope of three. Rob, generously says, "This is really nice climbing with someone competent!" Wow! But will I make it up the Matterhorn?

Lord Francis Douglas did the Trifthorn as a training climb in 1865, before falling off the Matterhorn with three others, when with Whymper. I try not to dwell on this. We discuss possible options, of starting at the Schonbielhutte and doing the Zmutt ridge, but this is too long and I fancy getting high to the Hörnli Hut and then ascending from there. It seems more straightforward and is going to be 4,000ft of climbing in five hours, hopefully, for the ascent. Same down. In truth I have gone off the whole idea, as am frightened of the mountain, though reluctantly I still want to do it...a sort of 'out of body' experience where I will go along with the idea and somehow just do it! Of course we are choosing the popular route where stories of frequent stone falls are scary for both of us. Lying in the soft grass in the sunshine, the dark black rock of a mountain seems an illusion. Noting my reluctance, Rob says, "I think we should go for it". Decision made.

I seem to share these feelings with others;

> *"The mountains one gazes at, reads about, dreams of and desires are not the mountains one climbs. These are matters of hard, steep, sharp rock and freezing snow of extreme cold; of a vertigo so physical it can cramp your stomach and loosen your bowels; of hypertension, nausea and frostbite; and of unspeakable beauty."* (Robert Macfarlane *Mountains of the Mind)*

Back in the valley I go to my room at the Bahnhof, and pinned to the door is a note *"Pieter Harper kommt Morgen um 11 Uhr ins Hotel*

M.A. and Peter on way to Hornli Hut

an." (Peter is coming to the hotel at 11 am). My son, Peter, who is climbing with his father at the Breithorn, is coming down to be with me. Hallelujah! I am emotional with joy. This masks my foreboding.

Peter turns up and we all go out for eggs and rósti on the terrace in the sun. This removes the imminent reality. So comfortable and relaxing! It turns out that Peter intends to come with us to the Hórnli hut. What a difference this makes for me. Rob and I shoulder our heavy packs and make for the lift up to Schwarzee with Peter, then Peter takes mine. This takes us up to 8,202ft and we only have another 2,559ft to the Hórnli Hut.

At the Hórnli we pull everything out of the rucksack and strictly ration ourselves as to what goes back in. Out goes hat, in goes headband, torch, anorak, scarf, crampons, axe, sunglasses and do I really need three pounds of chocolate? Water. Huddling round crowded wooden tables in the hut, it seems all very cheery, lots of laughter and I wonder what is wrong with me? I try to swallow the chicken fricassee but my throat is tight with fright. We meet other guides and one eighty-year-old, Dickie, who wants to try again. He failed last time. He climbed the Cioch on Skye this summer. This is humbling, and I hide my fears. I am 54. Peter and I go outside the crowded hut and sit quietly on a bench in the starlight. It is silent out there away from the bustle and heat of the hut. Just us and the Matterhorn above. And I will go up there tomorrow.

Wedged on the *matrazenlager* (sleeping shelf found in huts, where people sleep side by side, usually one shelf on ground level, and one above) between a snoring Italian and my son, sleep evades me. But at least I am resting my body. The Italian sticks his elbows in my back. I find tears are trickling down my cheeks at being so close to my son, and about to face the mountain! I am scared. Will I make it? Will I actually try?

Pre-dawn we get up, Rob and I, it is 3.15 a.m…dry bread and Nescafe and at 4 a.m. we are off, speed is vital. "Achtung", a German trips over my pack near the door, in the dark, nearly knocking me off the chair. Out the door. Turn right. Lights flash up ahead, lots of German voices call out, "Wolfgang, wo bist du!" We overtake four parties in the dark, the head torches lighting up a tunnel of light ahead. I have to route find, and it's tricky in this area of indistinct ground. I am sweating in fleece trousers, *Lifavest* and T-shirt. It's getting lighter, but moving together we keep going fast. It's a relief when we come to the Moseley slab and Rob decides to go up first and belay me…so that I get a break for five minutes. "M.A. you are climbing ace!" a compliment does help.

"Oh dammit Rob, I need to go to the loo." Nerves. What did Robert Macfarlane say? But I cannot take off my harness and let all those folk pass us again, so I hold on to it all for another six hours.

Past the Solvay Hut which we made in two hours flat, full of people who have bivvied there. I am aware of the ever-present risk of falling rocks from those people ahead but we are staying in front. The terrain is getting steeper and more solid and suddenly we are at the fixed ropes, rising up in front of us over snow and steep rock. Rob goes ahead. I tie on. I follow, it's *verglas* on the rocks and we have not put on our crampons, mine are in my pack. "M.A., you need your crampons here, lean out and place the soles of your boots flat on the snow, then put your crampons on, I am holding you." This from Rob, tied on the rope, some way above. I extricate my crampons from my pack, pulling it round so that it hangs off one elbow, don't drop it! Open the lid, and find them on top of my woolly hat, and somehow fix my pack back on my back and put them on. Heavens, I am only half way up the Matterhorn.

On way up mountain

I hang on to the strong steel spike at the top of the fixed ropes. It is so solid. Can I just stay here? Some people are already coming down, it is 8.30 a.m., is Peter having breakfast back at the hut? I let go of the spike…then forward and up over the snow slope to where Whymper's party fell. This was in 1865; they had just been the first people on the summit and on the way down four of the group fell down the north face. I don't think about the drop, 5,000ft from here past the Matterhorn Glacier to the Zmutt Glacier. I feel vulnerable with no axe, we had decided to take just one axe, which Rob carries, but most parties don't have an axe. I kick my crampons hard into the snow and the two front teeth bite in.

Zigzagging up we come to a large metal figure of a woman, which I found out later people use as a belay point. Rob told me that Madonnas are found on summits all over the Alps, but I have not done many Alpine peaks. We are on the almost horizontal narrow summit ridge, leading no doubt to the cross of which I had seen photographs, but when Rob asked, "Shall we go further along? There's a good path." A what? I looked past Rob and saw another vertical drop off behind him. "Sorry Rob, I can't." As far as I was concerned I had done it, I had climbed the Matterhorn. Definitely. I never did see the cross! But I did it! Here I was on the Matterhorn, aged 54, living out a lifetime's dream. One that been awaiting fulfilment since 1957.

M.A. on summit (Rob Collister)

Now we have to go down. The descent is horrendous, crossing the snow slope with just the one axe, I must not trip on my crampon straps, trying not to look ahead and down 5,000ft. We come to the fixed ropes and the spike where a queue of people is waiting to come up, but Rob insists we come down first. We are not popular, but there is not a lot they can do when we are occupying the fixed rope; *"Ach diese Enklander, sie denken nur an sich!"* (Thinking only of themselves.)

Moving fast, our crampons secure on rock and ice, then off with them, and on down the loose and crumbling ridge. We stay close to the edge of the ridge and I try not to think of the cold beer in the hut. Then I trip and land on my back on a pile of rocks. It could have been in a worse spot. Just dignity upset. Forget the beer.

We reach the hut, I drink my beer and then Rob said, "You must have been, well you were, a really good climber in your heyday." I suppose he was praising my efforts but I think that he felt I had managed the climb but that this was no longer a way of life for me. I had not climbed seriously for about 15 years. He was of course right! But I have this list of projects still to cross off, having had neither the time nor the money to do it when I was younger and having brought up my two children in the meantime.

We descend to the Schwarzee Lift, I feel so very anticlimactic and that Rob has finished 'another day at the office' as he is a professional guide. This is unfair but I guess this is how it is. I hope I thanked him sufficiently for being part of my big dream, for without Rob I would never have done it. It was the casting out and end of the dream I have entertained for 34 years, a hollow feeling of but what next? I should have been euphoric, but I was drained! Gaston Rebuffat wrote in his book, *'Starlight and Storm'*, that "Of our dreams are born the great joys of life. But one must have dreams." I suppose without them we would strive for nothing, but of course, once achieved we must find another.

In later years when I look at the Matterhorn, I find it hard to believe I did actually go up that ridge and sit on the top. It had been an image for so long, it is hard to convert it to a realisation.

My Last Munro: Buchaille Etive Beag, 26 August 1995

Last stone, last cairn Buchaille Etive Beag

"He travels fastest who travels alone."

Kipling, *'The Winners'*

My good friend Marjorie Langmuir had hers, Alan Keegan had his, and now it's mine...THE LAST MUNRO...I needn't climb another hill, and I won't get into Corbetts! No. Hamish Brown once told me I would find finishing my Munros an anticlimax, and he was right...nothing more to get up at dawn for, to drive for three hours to some obscure point on the map, mount the bike for a ride in...and then haul myself up a slope and along a ridge, often returning to the car about 10 or 12 hours later. Tired but happy. All done!

This would have been my father's 99th birthday, and I was conscious of making this day special to me. I had planned this modest hill, as it was possible for my sons in Edinburgh, friends in Aberdeen and Aviemore, to get together for the weekend. It mattered. My son Peter came just before heading for the Antarctic, Eric Langmuir and daughter Cate, leading orienteerer Carol MacNeill who read a poem on the top, Issie Inglis rushed over having just finished a Yachtmaster's course, and others included Janet Waller, my other son Angus, Peter's wife Stephanie, and solo climber Jules Lines. Peter and I skinny-dipped in the Etive on the way back to the bothy at Laggangarbh, which we had rented from the SMC for the night! There we all enjoyed a rich repast, laced with toasts of whisky, and much happy, convivial chat.

Reading Carol's poem

Stephanie on way up

Sharing champagne
with Angus

For me, I felt that only at my wedding had I felt special like this, that these people had turned out just for me! And for that I wanted to give a humble and heartfelt thanks, and I was sorry that some who wanted to come and couldn't, were not there...old Eric Furness, who bravely tried, aged 90.

This day was the culmination of many years of 'Munro bagging' as some would have it...I started seriously about 1983 and so enjoyed laying out the Munro map on the floor of the sitting room, and planning where to go next. Some areas, like Kintail, or

Glenshee, offer handfuls at once! Others, like Seona Braigh, or the solitary Cuillins, like Sgurr Mhic Choinnich, which I had to try twice, as it is so seriously exposed, take longer and require more effort. Long 14-hour days like the time I went along the Grey Corries, Stob Ban, and over Aonach Mor and Aonach Beag before thrashing my way back to Fersit and my car. Later I went back and did the Aonachs with Angus… great country.

I did most of these alone. I found it easier not having to find someone who wanted to do the same mountain, on the same day. I just spread out the map, and decided to go. I could get up at four in the morning and drive. I could also do a 12 or 14-hour day, pushing myself on and on to 'get them done and sit and put my toes in a stream,' I rarely stopped for a break. I suppose with no one to talk to there is little point, unless to take in the view.

I loved 'doing the Munros' and often defended myself against the taunting jibes of those 'not into them' by saying how much I had enjoyed getting to know Scotland, my country, parts of which I would still never have found, and had so enjoyed learning of the obscurer parts. Glen Clova springs to mind, Strathcarron and the wonderful peaks of Kintail, Torridon, Quinag.

Some mountains stay in my mind. Climbing Ben Lawers by moonlight, feeling spooky in the shadow of the hill, while the moonlight lit up the open slopes, and I sat on top and looked down on the lights of Loch Tay. Wonderful. The Fannichs, using my fingers spread out to stick in the snowslope in front of me (I had forgotten my axe)…and then traversing the range in the mist, when two well intentioned mountain men warned me to 'be careful' in the lack of visibility, on my own of course! I found I had become spot on at timing and navigation.

As Wilfred Noyce wrote in *'South Col'*, *"It was my first experience quite alone on the mountain, and I looked forward to it. To be sometimes alone is to be almost a physical necessity, for then the imagined shapes of the hills seem to speak, as they cannot do when another person, however sympathetic, is present to blur the contact. Solitude enlarges the nervous personality heightens perceptiveness. Terrors are then more acute, so also is the sensation of being a part with hills, and through them with all natural forms."*

The Great Out Doors Challenge

Or the Ultimate Challenge as it was initially called. Instigated by Hamish Brown and sponsored by Ultimate Equipment, I had heard of it, and indeed Hamish was coming to spend a night in my house in Aviemore on his way through, and was meeting a friend who would accompany him for a few days. Well, his friend arrived and unpacked her sack to show what she had taken. Hamish took out half of it and I had to send it back to her home!

Later on, I was to learn the same lessons, as I decided I would give it a go as well. I entered on my own in 2000, but would walk some of it alongside friends Anne and George Leggatt, and Alan Keegan from Speyside. Half way up Glen Affric I decided to make my own way, and said I would meet them again in Braemar. But there I met Mark, and continued almost to the end with his party.

Basically the TGO Challenge, as it is often known, runs each May, and it is a long distance walk from the west to the east of Scotland, starting anywhere really between Torridon and Ardrishaig and finishing on the east coast between Fraserburgh and Arbroath, a distance of some 200 miles. Initially one could take a high level route, or a low level one, but now it tends to be a mix. Usually about 300 people take part, and although it is definitely not a race, the people will all be walking within the same two week period, and it is rigorously monitored by those at base, so that one must phone in four times to provide a check on where one is. It is rugged, but the best bit is meeting so many good tough people, and in following years these become good friends. You may meet on a pass, or on a track, then perhaps take off on a different route, to complete your own individual route. The route is your own, but has to be vetted by base before you depart, making sure it is viable, and the vetters will warn of a bridge down or felled forest. The end is a party in Montrose, a celebration of sore feet and backs.

I walked this seven times, from different spots and it was on this trip I was lucky to meet up with Mark with whom I was to walk the John Muir Trail. A fortuitous meeting. Since then my knees and a bad ankle have made me reluctant to push for more. Tempted though I am, for it is fun to haul all this stuff – tent, sleeping bag, stove, and food across heather and peat hags and rivers, and camp in the wild in the open free Scottish hills.

CHAPTER FOUR
Long Walks

The Volcanoes of Ecuador and the Galapagos, 2000

I regularly climbed to 18,372ft each year as a trek leader in the wilder reaches of Nepal, so when I anticipated having a go at the volcanoes of Ecuador and read the trek company's advice, *"good peaks to gain high altitude experience and, given good conditions, are very attainable"* I felt that, although their summits are over 19,000ft I stood a fair chance – as I was *'fit and determined, with good acclimatisation records and competence on snow'*…how wrong I was.

We started with an acclimatisation trek around 13,123ft – memorable only for the pathless struggle through deep mud, balancing on tussock grass, sheltering from a cold wind and drizzle and spending hours in the tent in my bag trying to keep warm. It was too cold to read, and our days were too short, but good from an acclimatisation point of view. We did have a stretch along a lake below Artisan when the sun shone briefly through the cloud, but later that day a short, sharp gale lifted our hooped, unoccupied, tent high above the campsite and we nearly lost it. It got caught on a bush sticking out of the cliff!

I had decided to come to Ecuador with my friend Moira Langmuir. Her aunt had died of cancer and left me £5,000, which I decided to use to go to Ecuador and the Galapagos; as Marjorie was an inveterate traveller I thought she would approve.

We planned to climb Cotopaxi, Chimborazo and Cayambe – quite a daunting trio and perhaps, rather like some of my clients, whom I mentally accused of the same thing, I was guilty of not reading the brochure properly. It was very relentless. In one week we stayed in three refuges, did three night ascents, with two days off during this time to recharge the batteries in the sunny market towns of Banos and Otavalo.

We began with Cotopaxi, which at 19,347ft is the easiest of the three, and is climbed frequently by tourists in Quito, who hire a guide and go. My diary reads, *'Slowly I emerge from the depths of my warm bag, around me bodies grunt and scrabble after a torch. It is 10 p.m.*

and time to get up. We are all spread out on the floor in this high roofed hut. Staggering speechless, no jokes now, we don thermals, salopettes, harnesses – the duvet jackets and head torches come later – find ice axes and crampons, gloves and sweeties. Not like an Alpine Hut this, no friendly chat, and smell of coffee wafting from the Guardian's kitchen. (Think Hornli Hut on the Matterhorn!) We are alone here.'

Breakfast, which we cook ourselves, is a silent affair of porridge, muesli, toast and jam and lots of Nescafe. Then we blunder outside, it is a beautiful night, full moon and no wind. The lights of Quito are spread out below and occasionally a flash of lightning breaks through the clouds beneath us, as a storm plays itself out not far away in the jungle.

At 12.30 p.m. we set off from the Refuge. I feel fit and well and strong, no need for a torch in the moonlight. We notice Cassiopeia and Scorpio above us as our crampons crunch into the hard snow. I am enjoying this – huge deep crevasses and seracs open up in shadow alongside us in the moonlight – the rhythm of moving on a rope stepping in time to the one in front. Torchlight on the snow up ahead.

After about two hours everyone passed us, for there were more folk coming up this popular mountain, and the others had all disappeared around a corner. I was left alone on the mountain with my guide, Heime, who said, "You and me alone in the world." In many ways it was wonderful to be alone, with the mountain, the stars and the crevasses, but also, I suppose there was doubt that I would actually make it. This was the first time I had ever been overtaken on the hill, and it was an interesting feeling!

For a while it went fine – Heime was patient and I kept persevering until the snow went powdery and the axe wouldn't hold and my feet slid backwards (like ascending a scree slope) and I became more and more breathless. Heime said: "steady and slow," and for a while I did try, then I realised that even if I did make it, I would be far behind the rest, so decided to go down, to conserve my strength for the descent, and to be in charge of myself. Heime was so supportive and told me of the time he had pulled out of Huascaran, at 22,205ft the highest mountain in Peru, because he was too tired to continue.

Back to the refuge to wait four hours for the others, spartan in the extreme, steel framed bunks with two inch foam to lie on, no blankets. I lay back with a mattress for a pillow, my plastic boots propped at the end, and my duvet jacket over me and tried to sleep, but wind was rattling the windows and it was far too cold. The others turned up at nine absolutely knackered, but they had done it and I had not.

So next up was a break in Banos, which turned out to be a possibly final few days. Someone took us to a bar to sample a *pisco* sour. (For the uninitiated this is a South American staple...made of *pisco*, a base liquor, and mixed with lemon juice, it is strong and delicious!) We were then dragged off to another place where a competition ensued. I was told one of the group ended up dancing on the table, but I had gone outside to sober up, and sat down against the wall, to be joined shortly afterwards by Moira. Someone asked us if we needed help, and we did. We could not remember where our hotel was or what it was called. And it was very late. These people guessed right and led us home. A stupid and dangerous relaxation from the mountains. We were lucky.

Back to our mountains. I decided not to attempt Chimborazo, at 20,561ft it is the highest mountain in Ecuador and a daunting prospect. We stayed at a slightly less cold refuge at 16,404ft. There is no heating in these refuges, and they have high roofs and the door seems to be left permanently open. Taking a walk up to look at the route the day before, I was astonished that such a mountain was in a trekking brochure, and not in a high alpine mountaineering brochure. The route starts up a glacier and then proceeds along a ramp above ice cliffs, then breaks up through crevasses to a ridge. I could see the ice shining on the slope in the sun. I was so glad that I had no desire whatsoever to attempt this. As it was, the four who tried turned back because of high winds, rock hard ice and the thought that arresting a fall was therefore impossible.

I decided to attempt Cayambe, at 18,996ft a lower peak. Psychological? As I lay in bed before breakfast at 9 p.m. (remember, we climb at night!) and listened to the wind howling round the hut, my immediate thought, as a leader and Scottish hillwalker, was "it's not on". But we went. It wasn't too bad, with us all staggering upwards with the wind knocking us sideways, and the guides cutting snow profiles with increasing regularity, as this mountain is known to be very avalanche prone. Again I turned back, through complete breathlessness at 16,000ft, with one other person this time. Sadly the others didn't make the top as new snow had made a snow bridge really unstable, and they were unable to cross the *bergschrund* to the rock beyond. A vital link to the top. As one person said: "I didn't travel 8,000 miles to go out and have a day like Scotland in winter!'

I was hugely impressed with the Ecuadorian guides, so professional, so careful, kind and friendly and really efficient. The mountains are hard. The weather is difficult, and Cayambe is known to be windy and dangerous for avalanches, but given the weather they're certainly worth a shot. Ecuador is an amazing place with the coast, the *paramo* (Alpine tundra), the jungle, the glaciers and volcanoes all reasonably close together. One of the unusual aspects of this trip was that we could drive to the bottom of each volcano, requiring no long march in.

Moira and I then went off to the Galapagos, and joined a backpackers' boat, which was freezing. But we had fun and enjoyed scary swims with the sea lions, and stepping over the blue-footed boobies on land.

Hiking the John Muir Trail in California, 2001

Liberty Cap in Yosemite

"I went to the woods because I wished to live deliberately, to front only the essential facts of life and see if I could not learn what it had to teach, and not, when I come to die, discover that I had not lived..."
John Muir

As we put our gear together in the Yosemite Valley, a guy stumbled into camp, his face wrapped in bandages, and a big black bruise on his forehead. "Yeah", he said, "I met a bear. I went out in the night to relieve myself, but I had no flashlight, and surprised a bear eating my rations. He lashed out at me!" I guess he was lucky, or silly. We had been told we must use bear barrels on this walk, which severely restricted what we could take. We could only carry one each, with our food crammed inside. He had not taken one and had hung his food up a tree. The bears thought they were lucky...and with no torch he must have scared the bear.

John Muir was born in Dunbar in 1838, and after emigrating to the US with his very religious family, and settling in the west, he found himself in the Yosemite Valley, drawn by nature and simplicity to devote his life to preserving this, *"mountain mansion where nature had gathered her finest treasures"*.

In a history story too long to enter here, and a lot written up in *My Summer in the High Sierras* he became influential in co-founding the Sierra Club, that powerful conservation body, of which he became President in 1892. Yosemite Valley had been made a National Park in 1890, but under State control. In 1903 he took President Roosevelt deep into the backcountry of the Park where the President was so influenced by the beauty he experienced that he said it should be put under Federal control. (Yellowstone had been named the first National Park in 1872).

Muir was influenced by Emerson and wanted to live simply*, "carrying only a tin cup, a handful of tea, a loaf of bread and a copy of Emerson"*.

The John Muir Trail was named in his honour.

I had dreamed of this walk for over twenty years, when I must first have seen some photographs of it, and now here I was. Finding a partner who would do it with me was the catalyst. I had met Mark on the Great Outdoors Challenge across Scotland, and put it to him. He was keen.

Firstly a fun few days in San Francisco, buying food and riding the Cable Car at night. "We're on a mission, let her go," said the driver as he let her fly down the rails while we hung on, laughing at the sheer fun and freedom of all this. Ice creams at Ghirardelli's and the sea lions on Pier 22, where they cluster on floating ramps, hundreds of them. A fun and happy time, also getting to know one another. It was looking good.

I think nothing prepares you for arriving in the Yosemite Valley. 'El Cap' soars skywards and the massive hulk of Half Dome lurks in the backdrop. Although it is a bit of a turn off to be here in August when there are cars, shuttle buses and burger bars. But here we pick up our permits to enter the wilderness, and rent the obligatory bear barrels. These secure food containers have locking lids to prevent bears stealing the contents. Tourists drop food and leave it in their tents. In the past there have been so many incidents with bears, who have had to be darted and taken far off to another area, but the rich pickings bring them back. So now one has to take a bear barrel and the bears have learnt and so there are fewer prospecting in the higher areas.

Perhaps all this busyness makes our departure for the wilderness more poignant.

We were four, Tom and David, who were brothers, and fancied the walk but not to the same extent as Mark and I. We were committed. We had camped in the Backpackers' Camp at Happy Isles, below Royal Arches. I had climbed in this awesome granite theatre some years previously, on Royal Arches itself. I strayed alone into the quiet of the boulders and trees to absorb something of the overwhelming grandeur of this place. As I sat on a large rock I wondered how this experience would be.

We rose at five, while it was still cool, the threatening heat had not yet climbed over the peaks and penetrated the valley. We hiked 3,000ft upwards with packs weighing around 35lb in heat of 110 degrees Fahrenheit. It is a very tough start and perhaps the hardest part of the whole trail but it is stunningly stark, with Liberty Cap towering over you. A vast smooth grey granite cone. At the top of this purgatorial ascent there is a river with a huge pool. Dump pack and boots off – plunge in and float – splash! Delicious.

Dragging ourselves out and still wonderfully wet for a few minutes, we plough on through sand under a frying sun. The rock slabs absorb more heat, so the air is very dry and we drank pints of water from our Camelbak water bottles. (We purified all our water through a filter for the whole trip, as *giardia* is endemic here. This parasite can lodge itself in the intestine and causes severe diarrhoea until dealt with.)

That night we slept out on a rock slab, high above the Merced River, gazing up at a wide sky littered with stars and the lights of San Francisco-bound passing aircraft.

To convey the journey through to the end is difficult, but what stays with me is the space and incredible, tangible silence and the absolutely stunning scenery, constantly changing. There are twisted orange-barked pines, deep blue skies, frost on the grass steaming in the early sun, trout in the lakes and spots of deep blue water scattered across the valley floor, for the landscape is dotted with lakes.

We had long days, often 12 hours and covering 15 miles and almost always climbing 3,000ft. Rising at 5.45a.m., downing coffee and half a mug of instant porridge before starting out about seven and being on the next pass by 11, after which it became really hot. There are eleven passes to cross and 223 miles to cover and we estimated we climbed up, and down, about 40,000ft. The highest pass is 13,120ft but one is mostly hiking and camping at around 10,000ft.

The days were full of wonder and variety and about four days into the walk we took the chance to unload our packs and repackage the inner tent, trainers, and extra trousers and excess things and post them on to Los Angeles where we would be at the end of the trip. Fifteen pounds less weight! Here we indulged in a wonderful breakfast of pancakes, maple syrup and coffee and prepared to finish this section at Vermilion Resort.

My diary records that the next morning,

> 'I left early again and had an hour before the others caught up. I love this time alone. My friend, Jane, was right, four is too many, it is not a fragile number in this sensitive place. Hugely frustrated, I long to go on, but the boys want to hang out and go swimming…is this a priority…bide my time and stuff a hot dog, churlishly, down my throat. But I know we have to pass the afternoon but I can see the JMT slipping away and am cross and want to be upfront about it. This really matters to me – I am determined to do it – alone and on granola bars and water if necessary'.

That night George and Anne Leggatt, walking friends from Carrbridge in the Spey Valley, turned up at 8 p.m. as we were finishing dinner. Having scoured the campsite looking for us, they brought friendship, a bottle of wine and some Kettle chips. It was wonderful to see them. They impressed us with tales of climbing Mount Whitney in 14 hours and having a 23-mile day. We hope to climb this at the end before we descend to Whitney Portal.

We came eventually to Lake Edison, here you can take a boat to the end of a lake, to Vermilion Resort, where there are cabins, showers and a small shop. This is where we intended to pick up our resupply of more couscous, pasta, sauces and coffee which we had posted on ahead. You can swap tales with fellow walkers here, for you will meet few on the trail, mostly because you are all travelling in the same direction.

At this point Tom and David decided they had had enough and said it was too hard and they were off to do something else. So Mark and I repacked our rucksacks, my diary again, *'stripping our food down to ten days of supplies, we have one tea bag a day, two spoons of coffee, one slice of bread each, twenty snack bars (two a day or half a bar twice a day!) We bought some processed cheese, ham and 25 slices of rye bread.'* Apart from the weight, we cannot cram any more into the two bear barrels we carry. Then we are off along the lake to make an early start up Bear Creek Ridge the next day.

'Off at 6.45 a.m. because we have to go up 4,000ft today. Slabs and lovely pools. We feel very alone on this section. There are so many day hikers on the first part but a lot of people pull out at Vermilion. We meet a fat guy who says, "You are cruisin' – I sure would hurt something if I did 15 miles a day." We feel fine but it is raining now and we cannot camp where we want to because some wild lads are shooting guns into a lake.'

We continue, *'Cold at night, with lots of frost. Pan and sponge are frozen together. The sun always comes out. Meadows with steam rising off water. Sapphire Lake, high and wild and bare and open. Stopped at a small lake for lunch. Leaning against a huge rock, gear strewn across the grass to dry off. Mark is growing a moustache! We do not care. Hair*

Evolution Lake

71

washing and shaving belong to a different time. A peregrine swoops past us.'

Next is Muir Pass, at 11,955ft, it has a hut dedicated, to John Muir, erected by the Sierra Club in 1930. It is; *"intended as a temporary shelter for hikers caught in storms on this exposed section of the trail"*. This was a very open wild spot, with a pristine lake, Wanda Lake, nestling below the rocks.

In a camping spot, we came upon two men both of whom were Rhodes scholars, one from New Zealand and one from South Africa. We camped with them for three nights, and I bartered one double granola bar and one Snickers bar for two batteries for John's camera. We will keep the goodies for Mount Whitney. I even cooked up some griddlecakes with jam to share, then as I spilt the sauce for our supper, made up pesto to mix with pasta and couscous. I did not finish my supper.

Now it was very cold and I wished I had more clothes, but we walked in long johns and shorts and used socks for gloves, so were fine. Tonight it's *'quinoa and dried beef, which tasted like dishcloths, but sorted with curry sauce made up from a packet'*. Our food seems to get worse and worse.

Next an historic day; Wednesday, 12th September. On a cold and windy day, we left our big packs lower down and breathlessly started our ascent of Mount Whitney at 14,491ft. We met John and Stewart from Edinburgh, whom we had met previously. They were coming down and told us of, "A horrendous disaster of two planes flying into the two World Trade Centre Towers". You can imagine here that folk were listening to their phones, this seemed initially to have been an accident and the truth of 9/11 did not quite come out here.

We shared a Snickers bar and a Hershey bar with our friends, the Johns. Then started off down the 6,000ft to Whitney Portal. Endless zigzags for 11 miles but a note pinned to a tree from Anne and George from Carrbridge really lifted my spirits, "Message for M.A. Harper arriving around 12 Sept. We've been here, seen it, done it. We all made the summit yesterday…we'll hear all about your trip back home. Love George and Anne".

It was anticlimactic to finish, though I had lost a stone in three weeks!

Next day we got a run in a pick-up to our rented car and drove, somewhat silently, to Los Angeles, where Mark's wife was due to meet him, but of course there was a major hiccup as some planes did not fly after the horror of New York, others went by Toronto, and avoided New York altogether.

And so what had been a magical and life enhancing walk through the most sublime terrain imaginable dissolved into uncertainty and despair; my own at losing the companionship I had so relished over the previous weeks as we were about to return to our own separate lives, and the world's as the appalling events of 9/11 unfolded to foretell new uncertainties and confusions.

The world was upside down and I did not know if I would get my plane back to the UK. I was on my own.

I made enquiries at the hotel desk and eventually got to the airport for the KLM flight. There was a massive queue but the staff were hugely helpful, and we got on. The crew looked shocked and relieved to be leaving the US. We were one of the first planes to make it out. Dream accomplished.

Rae Lakes

Hiking the Wind River Range, Wyoming, 2002

Mike on trail with Squaretop behind

We watched fascinated as three goosanders herded fish into a corner of the lake, water flying up from wings and feet, just as whales herd fish in the ocean. A feeling of euphoria overtook us. No big pack on this day, just a daypack and a fishing rod! Exploring high up into this area of high blue lakes, towering rock walls and spires was wonderful. There were many 'erratics' here, signs of glacial times that carved out this basin, for this is the Titcomb Basin in the Wind River Range. Rocks were strewn over the slabs, like so many marbles tossed by a giant. People also come here to climb Fremont Peak, which is not technically difficult at all. (If you are a rock climber that is). And there is the addition of the Twins Glacier high up at the head of the Basin, which reminded us that this was high mountain terrain. The wind was blowing a bit and it was cold, so I crouched down behind a rock and nibbled on my cheese and crackers.

I had first heard of the Wind Rivers back in 1975, when the Cirque of the Towers was the 'in' place to climb. The Mountains here lie north of the Great Divide Basin, which is north of Colorado, south of Jackson and Yellowstone and bang in the middle of western North America. It is not easy of access! The stunningly impressive granite spires and towers are a constant backdrop as one winds one's way over and through the many passes and pristine blue lakes. Mostly one is above the tree line at 10,000ft in wild, stark country.

The Wind Rivers Range ('Winds' for short) runs for about 100 miles from the NW to the SE down the western side of the Continental Divide. It contains more than 40 named peaks over 13,000ft and seven of the largest glaciers in the Rocky Mountains are found here. It forms part of the Bridger Wilderness, named after an American mountaineer, Jim Bridger, who lived in the area during the early 1800s. He was a famous trapper and mountain man who went on to found a fur company to rival the Hudson's Bay Company. He was also the first white man to see the Salt Lake, which he thought was part of the Pacific Ocean as the water was salty.

I had heard access was a problem. Even getting to Pinedale, which is the gateway on the west side of the range, is not easy. We took a taxi south from Jackson, which is 59 miles and then a taxi in to the trailhead at Green River Campground, which lies amidst lofty pine trees surrounded by sultry meadows.

Mist hung lightly over the lakes and a ghostly canoe floated quietly on the surface, while the massive hulk of Square Top Mountain dominated the direction we would take today to start our exploration up the Green River and into the wilderness. Funny how rising at five or six a.m. becomes something one really wants to do when in wilderness country, it is such a shame to lie in, I think one likes to be part of the life stirring all around. The birds, the scuttling mice, and the jays. The walking was easy and gentle and there was a pervasive peace of leaving it all behind and entering into the simple world of a tent, some food, a trail to follow and silence. We were a small team of four, Jane, Neil, Mike and me. It is a strange feeling when the silence is so overpowering, even the slip of a boot sole on gravel is loud, and makes one want not to speak, to shatter this silence.

Our journey on the third day took us above the tree line and into the peaks, up boulder granite blocks and a rough trail, which would be hard if one was not fit and acclimatised. We were carrying food for a week, and camping gear and our packs were heavy. Nearly 40lbs each. The superb grandeur of the area and of Peak Lake sunk deep in a rocky basin, made us forget the weight we were carrying.

Titcomb needles

Strolling on, high above the world, with the Titcomb Needles on our left, forming a wall, we took a break for lunch and Mike and Neil tried a cast with new rods. I lay against a rock and gazed up at a clear blue sky and the grey rock and munched some nuts. We were high on happiness and space. There was no one here but us and the liberation was awesome. The fish did not bite. Perhaps we had the wrong lures or techniques. I felt very content and at peace with all life here.

We came next to the Titcomb Lakes area, which is a side valley off to the west of the trail. We camped amidst large rocks on a flat grassy sward by a lake, which caught the golden light of the low evening sun and reflected the frosty granules on the stems of grass in the morning. We cooked up some pasta and opened a jar of pesto. Food in the outdoors takes on a different feel to that taken in the home, just basic things…pasta, soup, veggie stew or spaghetti with tins of sauce are perfect…one is outdoors, sitting on a rock, one can breathe in the openness of a wide sky, cliffs and water, then a bald eagle soars past. No traffic, no phones, no people. No timetable. Perfect. Just grass or a rock to sit on, no compulsion to 'do' anything, just experience the letting go, and wanting to live this way for ever.

Resupply day had come, and we had to follow a track to Elkhart Park to where we had arranged for our resupply to be delivered. Strange and amusing day passing poodles with panniers on their backs,

Lake in Titcomb Basin

hopefully carrying their own suppers. We even met a man taking in a horse to carry out a man with blisters, who wanted out. Expensive blisters. We dipped in and out of 'people'.

We were entering a new area now, which became much more interesting and challenging, as it is between the Titcomb Lake area, which is much visited and the Cirque of the Towers, a climbers' paradise of granite slabs and spires. Our plan was to take an unused trail over an unnamed pass, but it was not on the map. Fortunately we met a guy with an old map, and we were able to pen our route onto our own. This trail had been removed from the map in 1987 as so many people got lost and had to be rescued. Not us, we are sure! Going up towards the peaks of Bonneville and Raid there was not a soul in sight, but a huge granite boulder field to stagger across for three hours, being careful not to trip with our large packs, with the knowledge rescue could take a while.

Stupendous stuff, descending over the pass into an unfrequented valley, with 2,000ft rock slabs dropping off to a lake. The path zigzagged down. Careful now. We met a couple fishing on the lake, and had no idea who was more amazed to see the other. This was the Cirque of the Towers I had heard so much about.

Entering the Cirque of the Towers

A flock of sheep up here was guarded by three Pyrenean Mountain dogs. Having nearly been eaten by a pack in Greece I was very wary, but they seemed friendly enough, and when we sat down one spent all his time licking my face, maybe I was a salt lick!

Pingora swept skywards, huge slabs of granite, as I lay on my back by my rucksack and watched two ants high up on the slabs. Lonesome Lake shimmered behind me, and I have this strange need to share the climb, to be there, to feel the rock on my fingertips and to balance and feel and check my belays. Holding my breath and being aware. Sensing the exposure, and ever present danger, how one must take care, pay attention, it can all go so wrong. There is no way I could climb that, but I do like to escape into the experience and lock myself in there. Instead, the sun shone down and warmed my knees, while I gazed through binoculars at the couple on the vertical slabs. Cosy and comfortable on dry friendly grass. Hot dry grass smells so good. We heard Fred Becky was in town, and had just climbed Pingora. He was a well-known name in the climbing world in the sixties.

We had organised a lift out from the Pinedale Cab Company. Never ceases to amaze me that these arrangements work out, to meet a taxi in the middle of nowhere at an appointed time three weeks hence, or more.

Trust is called for. The magic was slow to leave us as we watched a moose and her calf, refreshing themselves in the river by the track. Most dangerous animal? Maybe.

All adventures seem to end with a shower and a feast…in our case steaks and baked potatoes and wine, no sooner than it is downed, the anticlimactic feeling sets in and it's time to find another adventure.

Pingora

CHAPTER FIVE
Trek Leading

How I got into Trek Leading, 1987–2001

When people hear of all my adventurous trips around the world they usually ask how I got into this wild journeying. Luck? Partly...but I do not believe in that sort of luck. One does have to nudge oneself in the right direction first, then perhaps luck kicks in.

It is difficult to know where to start. I was an only child and had spent much of my life following a solitary path, a solitary adventure, in the hills, or across foreign lands. I loved wild places, and loved working with people whom I found stimulating and fun, if also madly irritating and frustrating at times when on trek. I was a mountaineer, having climbed in the Alps and Scotland, and I spoke French and German with smatterings of Spanish, and was used to teaching groups of people to ski, so organising groups was not difficult, but was rather different on a Cairngorms ski slope from at an airport or Himalayan pass.

A close friend of mine who was always taking off on trekking trips to far off spots knew how much I wanted to go there too and encouraged me to do so. I did not want to spend the little money I had, but I booked on a trip to Morocco, which was closer to home than Nepal, or Ecuador. So off I went and found myself in the Atlas mountains helping the leader erect tents, light stoves and cook meals...so I said to him, "How do I get into this?" he said, "Apply!" So I did.

Imagine my shock and delight when I was asked by Jim Reville, of Sherpa Expeditions to take a group to the High Level Route in the Pyrenees. Jumping in with both feet and despite never having been to the Pyrenees I accepted.

This was a story of a very tough 'survival course', so named by some of the group half way through, over the hills of Spain, with maps that did not match the terrain, (Spanish maps notoriously involve a lot of guesswork) and cooking for the group when we got down after 10 hour days. At the end of this, I caught a train to Martigny in Switzerland and arrived at the campsite to lead three groups on the Tour de Mont

Blanc. I was met by Graham who immediately informed me that, "M.A. you need to put these ten tents up. The group will be here later and then you can prepare the meal." The tents were Vango Force Ten which I could manage since we had used these at Benmore Centre, the Edinburgh outdoor centre in Argyll, where I had helped run camps for children from schools in the city.

So I started my career as a trek leader and I never looked back.

My next most memorable adventure was to be asked to take a group to the Everest region of Nepal. I had not been there either but, of course, I went! It was wonderful and I loved being out there, in the wild high mountain lands, with the Sherpas, the cook crew, yaks and porters. A seasoned leader, Anne Sainsbury, gave me lots of tips and lists and as our bus pulled out of Kathmandu to drive to Jiri, from where we would start our walk in to the mountains of the Khumbu and Everest, and to Namche Bazaar, I waved, and she shouted, "Good luck!" All these magical long dreamed of names…and now I was there.

After this I led many more trips in Nepal than I have included here. I have written about the poignant eventful ones, where the snow fell too much, or 'things' nearly went wrong, and when I had to evacuate someone with incipient pulmonary oedema at two in the morning. I have not said too much about the Everest region which I loved, the deep blue Gokyo lakes with the Brahminy ducks (Ruddy ducks) in the autumn, the smell of smoke in the air, the cries of boys driving the yaks, Ama Dablam rising up above the valley reaching to Pheriche near to Everest. This has to be my favourite mountain. I have written about Dolpo and Humla in western Nepal, and described the Mani Rimdu festival at Tengboche.

There are so many vivid snapshots in my head, of incidents and moments, of local children and marvellous Nepali women singing and giggling at five in the freezing mornings, making our tea…bringing 'bed tea' to our tent and a basin of hot water, to wash… *'Tato pani didi'*.. for they called me *'didi'* which is Nepali for 'older sister'.

Thereafter I led often in Morocco, Greece and Russia. I was also fortunate to lead trips into Tibet and visited Lhasa several times, but I found the Chinese influence and concrete buildings so depressing. At that time the Tibetans were still making the arduous pilgrimage to the Jokhang Temple in the centre of Lhasa. Pilgrims would prostrate themselves for months, until they arrived here at this special place and then turn round and go home the same way. So the Chinese have not stamped this out, yet. (Prostration involves kneeling down, and then stretching forward to lie flat...then bring the feet up and kneel and stand up again...and so on).

I was glad to lead to wild and remote places, Zanskar, Ladakh, Pamirs, with wild crazy helicopter rides, even Chechnya. I actually learnt Russian, writing down new words phonetically in a notebook so that I could communicate with our crew, albeit in short sentences. I walked round Mount Elbrus twice, the first time losing a camera containing film. The second time we walked round Elbrus I found a wee boy using my camera to take our photograph, the batteries were long dead but the film from the previous year was still inside. This was so extraordinary – there we were crammed into a lorry bumping along a rutted track, when I suddenly spotted my camera. I guess it was the surprise of the moment, but I regret to say that I paid 20 dollars to negotiate its return. I still feel bad that I did not leave the boy with the camera, it was such a mark of prestige, in a place where people had nothing.

So, this is the answer to the question of how I was launched into the exciting world of leading treks, which I did for about twenty years. I loved the challenges and the local people; in the Pamirs wild horses and yogurt from the nomads, and in Morocco the Berbers singing and giggling, and my son falling into a well in the Jebel Sahro and being fished out and dressed in a *djellaba* by the Berbers. It was an exciting, challenging life and I loved it.

Angus and the Berbers

Namaste, drama in Nepal at 15,700ft, 1996

Everest and the Khumbu Icefall

As a trek leader for Sherpa Expeditions I was fortunate to have already cut my teeth on leading a trek in the mountains in Nepal. I had already walked in from Jiri to Lukla, a lovely slow walk in past villages and barley fields, and then joined the normal trekking route to Lobuche and Kala Pattar, from where one looks on Everest. (The Everest Base Camp route.) I had also taken a group round the Annapurna Circuit which finishes off wandering down the wonderful wide open Kali Gandaki gorge, following small troupes of Tibetans, the smallest children carrying a frying pan on their backs. Maybe they were travelling with the yaks taking the salt south.

On the right was Dhaulagiri and to the left was Annapurna. These two giants face one another across the gorge, 20,000ft above it, towering giants, dripping with cascades of ice, or shining white snow. One felt very small on the wide alluvial plain, dwarfed by an overwhelming landscape. At the end is Pokhara with views over the lake to Machapuchare, or the Fishtail Peak.

The Kali Gandaki gorge is a major trade route between Tibet and India and, according to most calculations, is the deepest gorge on earth.

It was vitally important for the Tibetan salt trade, which bartered salt and barley for sugar and rice from India. Since I trekked the Chinese have built a new road all the way up the gorge. I felt my soul float here, to the high snowy peaks, and enjoyed trudging with the yaks carrying the Tibetans tents, giving their horns a wide berth! I can see the magic has not left me.

The trip I record here took in the wonderful lakes of Gokyo, which is a side trip between Namche Bazaar and Lobuche.

This time we were flying into Lukla, in a small twin Otter plane, holding perhaps 20 people. As I had walked in to Lukla last time, in 1987, I was not prepared for the landing. "Walls of mountains on the left, turn right, head for the ground, line her up and go. Brakes on, flaps vertical, we stopped – facing the mountainside." Hens scattered on the runway. We were at 9,403ft.

It always took a while to get going, sort out the loads between the porters and the yaks. There is general bustle, of course the clients are ready to go and anxious to move, but as leader I was always reluctant to leave until I knew we had all the bags. Although I slept badly on my first night, I enjoyed listening to the porters chatting under the rocks where they cooked their *tsampa,* the cook crew singing and clattering pots in the cook tent, the yak bells clonking and the Dudh Kosi roaring past below us. Whilst above us Thamserku's fluted slope glistened in the moonlight. It was always heart lifting to come back.

The wonderful, inevitable, bed tea arrives, at 6 a.m. or earlier. I used to have mine with the boys at five, standing at the door of the cook tent. The boys would come from the tent, one carrying a tin bowl with tin mugs rattling about inside it, as the other lad held the kettle with the tea. He would hand me an empty mug. There was usually another lad with the milk and sugar. *'Dudh? Chini?'* They called me *'Didi'* which is elder sister in Nepali. I am a MUCH older sister, but it's a friendly name.

This is followed by *'Washing watah'.* Another bowl and more hot water. A summary splash of the face, and one's private parts, follows! In that order. The towel is clean at the start, but after three weeks… I would try to check on it…or use my T-shirt to dry my face.

We proceeded up the trail, passing a wee hut with a tree and *'Lavatree'* painted on the side (in case you are slow as I was…

lavatory!) Then a long haul up to Namche Bazaar, which somehow always seems as if it's where it all begins.

Namche sits at 11,286ft and one does notice a shortage of breath heaving oneself uphill. This bustling little market town is built in a horseshoe shape contouring round the steep hills above the Bhote Kosi. There are two-storey houses, a bank and a number of stores selling anything from Star Beer to ice screws, and hats and sunglasses. Here one can eat pancakes, and spoil oneself a little, buy forgotten items or a thicker pair of gloves. More importantly one gets one's first view of Everest, Lhotse and the wonderful singular mountain, my favourite, Ama Dablam.

Usually one meets other groups and for me it is helpful to get first-hand information from another leader about the conditions for the next stage. In this case we are warned that temperatures where we are going are minus 28 degrees Celsius. Also there is a horrifying tale of three Japanese dying of High Altitude Cerebral Oedema (HACE) at Gokyo ten days ago. This is where we are going. I had a huge first aid kit, which was always carried by a Sherpa, so that we could get to it quickly. The contents were daunting – everything from plasters and Dettol, to aspirins, bandages and drugs. Drugs to cope with high altitude problems, heavy-duty diuretics and medication to help us to get someone down to lower altitude if they needed to. This usually alleviates the problems and after a few days one can reascend, this is easy to arrange in the Khumbu as there are so many tea houses along the way where a client and a Sherpa can spend a couple of days. The classic dictum is, 'climb high, sleep low' so that one should always try to ascend the ridge above camp before descending to sleep, as one gains altitude. I led about 18 treks in Nepal, so eventually I became quite conversant with the contents of the kit and even sneaked the occasional tranquilizer to get myself a good sleep when my mind buzzed with the ever present problems and obstacles of route and group. This was strictly against the rules at high altitude!

Next day we travelled on via Kunde and Khumjung, just beyond Namche. There were wonderful dry stone walls here and seemingly sterile earth. Sherpa women were working the ground with shovels like pick axes and there were hordes of children. The women wear long skirts and the kids wear ragged jackets and trousers, no doubt passed down from some charity shop. Frequently, the women tend the crops, potatoes and barley, as the menfolk are off working with treks or climbing. The name *Sherpa* means 'people from the east' and their history is that they were driven south out of Tibet by the Mongol hordes. They speak Tibetan as well as their own dialect, and dress in the Tibetan fashion.

We dropped in on Kunde Hospital and had a talk from the doctor there about high altitude medicine. This hospital was built by Edmund Hillary, who also built the first school in this area, in Khumjung in 1966. We were reminded to drink between 16 and 20 cups of tea a day in order to replace the fluid in the body lost at high altitude, to eat lots of garlic and to go slowly. I often found on treks, that the young fit guys suffered AMS, (Acute Mountain Sickness) whereas the older folk who plodded on slowly were fine.

This situation was to be borne out later. As a leader I would brief the group on all the above, but it was always nice to have it confirmed as often I heard, "I can't drink that much." To which the only response was, "Well, please try!" I consulted my friend, Peter Steele, a very experienced high altitude doctor, about this and he confirmed that the reason for dehydration at high altitude and its subsequent slide into HAPE (High Altitude Pulmonary Oedema) and HACE is the hyperventilation trying to cope with low oxygen pressures in the blood at this elevation.

It was snowing as we dropped down to Phortse Khola through juniper, birch and hanging moss, so I rigged up a tarp to provide some shelter while the tents were put up. The arrival of the yaks tip toeing down steps with large snow covered loads was a dramatic sight. I was not enjoying the Peapod tent, which was too small for this trip. The floor was wet so I put a Thermarest on top of my Karrimat, and slipped off its slippery cover all night! It was cold. Breath came in cloudy puffs of air inside the tent. I always loved the simplicity of living here, although sometimes the cold and the damp, would down one's spirits. Then the Cook Boy would run past shouting, "Breakfast Didi!" as he carried steaming bowls of porridge into the Mess Tent on a bamboo tray, and I was happy again, in my element.

Next day disaster. It was cold, and the trail was narrow and slippery. Suddenly a yak fell and descended 500ft to the river. He had a heavy load, the kerosene, which probably caused him to lose balance. The poor yak was killed, but we did retrieve the fuel, which we needed. This definitely put a damper on the day.

But from now on it's going to get tougher. This trail is very dangerous dropping steeply down, so I broke some branches from trees, which some nervous clients could use as sticks. I had my poles, but sometimes wondered at the wisdom of giving my safety equipment to a client, when the leader needs to stay alive. One could argue this both practically and morally.

Paul, from home, in Scotland, was constantly going ahead and asking me why we were so slow. I tried to tell him we need to avoid being affected by altitude. He was young, 34. I was glad to have him there, as it was so cold, minus 20 degrees Centigrade, and even though I am fairly tough and was sleeping in all my clothes and hugging my trek bag, I was frozen. Leaders sleep alone in their own tent, so Paul kindly suggested I joined him and Mark in their tent, and I was very cosy! What a difference.

The trail was hard. Desolate and barren, and I could not get air. I had to keep stopping. But the sight of the wonderful green lakes at Gokyo raised my spirits and restored some air to my lungs. Mist was rising off the water and there were two chestnut brown Brahminy ducks (Ruddy Shelducks) at the edge.

Gokyo at 15,700ft is a bleak settlement of stone houses and walls. Paul shot up the lateral moraine behind the campground and then ran down again for lunch! The rest of us staggered up later and gazed at Everest over the massive Ngozumpa Glacier, a huge body of ice, which at about 22 miles long, is the longest in Nepal. Of course the presence of this ice causes the temperature to plunge still further.

Next day we rose at 5 a.m. and started up Gokyo Ri (17,984ft). This is all part of the plan to help with acclimatization. It is not easy and not everyone made it, but from even half way up one can see across to Everest, Lhotse, Cho Oyu, Ama Dablam, Kang Taiga, Thamserku and more. Worth the effort, just, but it must have helped! Scattered group, heaving on air with the effort. There was a very cold wind and red, yellow and blue prayer flags fluttering off a cairn. I staggered down, tripping on rocks and grasping my poles.

Chatting at camp, as one does inevitably, about food...lunch came, tuna, chips, turmeric coloured cauliflower, bread and mango. There is lime tea, which we can't face, but we drink it, like good trekkers. Jean as usual picked at the bread, and rolled off a list of all delicacies she put in her Sainsbury's trolley, "I buy food, chicken, steaks, eggs, fruit…" We greeted this daily diatribe in silence. I struggled to get her to eat rice each day. Sometimes it's hard to be patient and polite, when someone like this can jeopardise the trip, by not eating, and getting weak.

Bedtime, early at 7p.m., was very hilarious watching Colin and David having their wash inside the tent with a torch highlighting their every move – creating a shadow theatre of funny silhouettes, an arm here, a leg there. I couldn't sleep at all. Paul was coughing and spluttering and it seemed that he might have fluid in his lungs. For about an hour I waited to see how he was, sitting up in the tent with him and Mark and leaning against the tent pole. I was so glad I was in their tent and knew what was going on. I tried the stethoscope but couldn't hear anything, then, he lay down and I heard three breaths like someone using a straw to blow bubbles in a glass of water. This is the classic tell-tale sound of fluid in the lungs. I said he had to go down, and he said, "No I will wait till morning". Leader stood firm. It was 2 a.m. "Out Paul, NOW." I woke up the cook crew and found Sirdar Mingma. Paul's stuff was packed and I handed him two Lasix, strong diuretics, to help get rid of the fluid in his body, should he need them, a cup of tea from the kitchen and at three he and Sherpa Jetta were off. The temperature was minus 22 degrees C but it was a clear night with a moon so they should be fine. I knew I that had made the right decision but was worried about other clients in other tents…could I 'sleep' in every tent?

Next day some folk went back up Gokyo Ri. I washed my hair in the lake and then, after I combed my frozen hair, brushed snow off my comb. Then we started down. The sun was shining. The mood has changed, group is in high spirits and kind and fun. Are we escaping? We hoped to catch Paul in Phortse, but there was no sight of him, he must have got further down, which is good. Instead we sat in the sun, watching an old lady dig up potatoes which we ate for lunch. An old man is mending a jersey. Juniper smoke hovers in a doorway. Here there are huge prayer wheels, which are turned by the water power of the river. A friend of mine from Aviemore turns up, he is taking a client further down, who is suffering from the altitude. He asks for some Dettol, the client has a cut finger.

Everyone is high on views of Ama Dablam. We visited the *gompa* in Pangboche. Lots of chanting and incense burning was in progress and we had to go upstairs to where the alleged Yeti skull and hand are kept. We slept in a lodge, and after lots of commotion getting mats on the floor to sleep on we played Trivial Pursuits in teams. Good fun. I got thrown out for knowing the answers…as I played it on every trip!

Then we headed up into the valley and camped at Pheriche and visited the Himalayan Rescue Association for another talk on altitude. I think we all feel a bit past this now, though I never stop keeping an eye out. I have two folk with bronchial coughs. This is 'Khumbu cough' which is common in the high dry air, and two more with peripheral oedema, when the hands and ankles swell with retained fluid. I took half a Diamox as I had it too, round my eyes, which were very puffy. Diamox is a recognised medication at altitude, it is a diuretic, and does help stop a build-up of fluid in the tissues. Most folk are pretty tired and it's still minus 18 degrees C.

I saw photographs of this desert area recently, and in 1953, there were trees everywhere. But during the course of time all the trees have been chopped down by the local people for firewood, until now they have to venture ever further for wood. I used to ask my clients avoid taking a shower as the water is heated by wood, creating further problems. Nowadays some places are putting in solar panels. Of course more trekkers mean more

Sherpa graves and Everest

money, more teahouses and more with windows, and more money to buy wood. It's a difficult one.

In Lobuche I put myself into a lodge to sleep, and actually had my first ever experience of Cheyne Stokes breathing, where you stop breathing, then take a big gulp of air suddenly and start breathing again. Very alarming for anyone near, but I woke myself up. Anyway, next day it was 'upwards and onwards' to Kala Pattar along the moraines coming down from Everest. I didn't make it, but fell asleep on a boulder and was only woken by someone asking if I was alright! "Yes, I am just the leader of this group!" Some set off for Base Camp, but didn't make it, "because we had no leader"…too bad. Even leaders get ill. They were a breakaway group, who decided to just do this as well, after KP.

Jetta has returned leaving Paul at Lukla to fly to Kathmandu. Later we learned that he had gone to the hospital, where he was found to have shadows in his lungs, but thanks to getting him out when we did, he recovered and did tell folk in Scotland I had given him a timely rescue. I sometimes think that as a leader one deals with life and death moments, but it is all part of the trek. It is serious stuff, and I think one becomes used to living at this level of apparent risk. I never lost sight of the possible threats of altitude sickness. I used to find, that when I had a client who was a doctor that just complicated matters, as I had to bow to their superior knowledge but often they had NO experience of altitude problems, whereas I seemed to deal with them daily!

But the trip was not over, another pass is advertised in the brochure, and three of them want to try, this pass, the Kongma La, links the Pheriche valley with the Chukkung one. "Tomorrow it's shit or bust," says Nigel. I am coughing so much and blowing my nose nonstop and it hurts. That night I 'sleep' sitting up against a wall. No Kongma La for me.

As a leader it is always so hard to make the right decisions, for the health of the clients and their safety, as often the leader can see how the situation can develop, whereas the client has 'paid for the holiday in the brochure' and expects to accomplish everything. I did have to take strong decisions sometimes which prevented clients doing what they imagined, travelling in a group bubble, they would do, whatever their health or the state of the mountains, but the companies that I worked for always backed me up to the hilt. I learnt early on in trek leading, not to discuss these problems and impending decisions. I would draw back into myself and usually, from assessing the situation in front of me, I would gain the strength, if necessary, to single people out and state my case strongly. If they died because I had given in to them, who would be held responsible?

It is hard to notice the mountains, but it was so beautiful going to Tengboche and to see the huge monastery there. We relaxed passing through the pink and white rhododendrons, red birches and hanging mosses. Smelling the grass. Ama Dablam does dominate, and I think this is one of my favourite places in Nepal. I must have taken dozens of photos of this mountain. Always just one more. Everyone is exhausted. Mark is walking so slowly, and I tried to find a lodge for him, but they are so cold. In the dining room it was warm but noisy, but in the end I got him a mattress and a yak blanket, and hope he will feel better tomorrow. It is always so humiliating for fit young men to be cut down by altitude. I saw it a few times, and some men find it too hard to deal with and dissolve in tears. It perhaps destroys all personal images of oneself, and is seen as personal failure, which of course it isn't.

Only minus eight degrees celsius now. Spirits are rising with the temperature. Mark is much better. Lunch was stew, cabbage, salad, chips, chapattis and fruit. Wind blew dust in our juice and behind the bazaar an old lady counted her beads and muttered her prayers: *'Om mani padme hum.'* Jetta cleaned his nails and Lakpa combed his hair. After Namche and a bit of strutting by the lads, it's off down to Phakding and Lukla comes soon. I met a friend of mine there, another leader, Val Pitkethly, and she and I sat on a wall drinking rum tea and coughing our guts out! This lubricated our throats and our chat. She is just back from Mera Peak, a trekking peak, with two Americans.

At the airstrip we found we would be delayed as no planes were coming in from Kathmandu. We would have to wait a day. So I organised a game of rounders on the airstrip. I found an old fence post for a bat and someone had a ball. In no time at all we had a huge audience, amongst whom was Sir Edmund himself! It was great fun and passed the time easily. Next day we flew out. But of course we had had our farewell dinner and cake, all dancing to the crew singing *Rissum piri ri.* As Colin said, "It's good for the Sherpas to see us making prats of ourselves!" They are so fluid and sinuous and we seem so clumsy. Big bodied, wearing our boots and with no idea of rhythm! It's always so sad going through so much together and dealing with all the problems and dangers and friendship and sharing, to just wave goodbye.

We enjoyed a good meal with the group in Kathmandu who gave me earrings but best was they said, "M.A. isn't our leader, she is our friend". That evening I was brought down to earth, far from Nepal. At the hotel I had a telegram from Peter, my son, telling me that a room had come up in a Home in Inverness and he had taken my mother there. She had Alzheimer's and since it was an ongoing problem for me to cover my absences, I had tried to find a place for her, but I was so grateful to Peter as it would have been very hard for me to take her myself from Edinburgh to Inverness, knowing she was leaving her home for good.

After they left I had a wonderful breakfast at Mike's, famous for his pancakes and maple syrup, and loads of black coffee, in a garden with many poinsettia trees. They made me think of the puny little plants we have at Christmas at home. Then I had to board the flight to London and Inverness, and when I got home I went to bed for five days, after all that I had flu.

Sometimes trek leading made me wonder, but I kept doing it! I loved the life.

Gokyo lakes in mist

Langtang and the Ibisbill, 1991

The Ibisbill, or Plumbeous Water Redstart, is related to the oyster-catcher and avocet, it breeds typically in south Central Asia on stony riverbeds typically between 5,600ft and 14,400ft. River valleys frequented by the Ibisbill tend to have very little vegetation but it must live near slow moving water in order to feed. It probes beneath rocks for insect larva and small fish. A grey bird with a white belly and red legs, I knew it would be hard to spot amongst grey pebbles. I had met someone on the trail in from Dunche in the Langtang Valley who had spoken excitedly of seeing the Ibisbill, so I had a mission.

I squeezed myself onto the bus from Kathmandu to Dunche along with Australians, Israelis and lots of locals for the ten and a half hour ride. We are all sitting three to a seat with lots of folk on the roof, this being the preferred place to travel.

I'm on my own, no clients! My small rucksack is under the seat. I hung on to the rail in front as the bus bounced and bumped over the rocky track.

We passed lots of *Chhetri* houses, thatched, slated and roofed in corrugated iron sheets. The Trisuli valley is very fertile; there are terraced rice paddies, bananas, papayas, buffalo, goats and hens, and lots of mynah birds, some egrets and a bittern. As we drove higher it began to pour and children, hens and goats were all sheltering under the balcony of the house. When we drew into Dunche (6,450ft) I bolted to the Langtang View Lodge where I shared a mixed dorm with 15 Israelis, but there was running water in the basin, and a tap. I ate noodles and egg fried rice and prepared for the trail tomorrow.

This is a birding trip. Black Drongo, Plumbeous Redstart, Cuckoo, European Nuthatch, all come out for my appraisal, as bird book in hand I stepped out. How different from the high Khumbu. This is a fertile valley, the wheat is well on, there are elaborately carved houses with geraniums outside, and ladies winding and weaving wool. I make my way up and down to the Langtang Khola, through forest and down a stepped path, through white and pink rhododendrons in glorious full bloom, oak and orchids.

After passing and repassing one another for a while, it seems I am destined to choose whether or not join up with Ruben from Israel and Geoffrey from the US. I do so; it's a comfortable threesome.

This low level trek was a delightful mixture of luscious, colourful vegetation gradually changing to open yak pastures, walled in fields with lots of *chortens* dotted about. I spot a mountain at last (am I missing the Khumbu!) Langtang Lirung (23,769ft), glistening white against a deep blue sky. There was lots of lying in the sun and my diary seems to record a diet of noodles, Tibetan bread and fried eggs to keep me fed and happy. There are more rhododendrons here, and daphne and many sounds from unseen birds, but I spot a Snow Pigeon.

Ibisbill next?

We ascend to the meadow at Kyanjin (12,300ft) and drop by the cheese factory, have a bowl of yogurt, then with Geoffrey in tow I head further up the valley towards the airstrip and along the bank of the Langtang Khola. First we noticed a couple of wagtails, then two Ibisbills, fishing under rocks. Mission accomplished. I was wildly excited, as this is a rare bird for me. That night we stayed at the lodge, which has a lovely wood burning stove in the centre of the main room. More noodles.

Now we just had to head back to Dunche but meantime we met a Welsh couple wanting to climb Langtang's trekking peak, Naya Kanga (19,160ft), but there is a lot of snow and skis are needed. I am so glad not to be doing that.

Heading down it is hotter each day and there is wheat being weeded and I spot irises at the edge of the field. We stay at Bamboo Lodge, a magical spot where there is an old lady, with a baby on her back, sweeping the yard. There are monkeys in the trees nearby and another Plumbeous Redstart and a Golden Oriole, I thought. I went down to the river for a wash, sitting on a big rock. This is great, it is lovely to sit outside amongst the chickens and hens and cat and kids. Granny is asleep on a bench and two wee kids are kissing mum while she cooks the rice. Grandad is asleep too. We are indeed privileged to be part of this private family life, and it feels very special indeed. There is a low-slung bamboo roof over our heads, and a thin bamboo partition between our beds and their family circle.

My two friends, Geoffrey and Ruben, have been good trail mates. Ruben and I have connected so well and shared some wonderful moments, which goes to show sharing and understanding has nothing to do with age, as he is only 20 and I am 51. We love listening to the wind in the trees, the bees buzzing in the wonderful silence of the moss covered conifers, and the river tumbling down over rocks. I appreciate that they pushed me the way that I like and we often had long, long days of nine to ten hours. I reflected how sad it is at the end after all this time together…it's merely, "bye, thanks", then we split, and I go on down to Langtang View Lodge to meet a new lot of green trekkers.

This is the story of trekking life, meet and part and start again. Not easy and one must come to terms with the transitory nature of these friendships but enjoy them at the time for what they are and what they give. Then move on.

I rode back to Kathmandu on the roof of the bus. To pick up my next group, of new trekkers, to walk the Annapurna Circuit.

The Caucasus and climbing Mount Elbrus, 1991

Returning to the Priut

The huge station in Budapest is overwhelming. Enormous behemoths of engines spew thick smoke from their funnels, huge steel wheels grind on massive rails, and trains shunt and groan. No diesel trains here! It is also dark. One feels one is entering a whole new world, or going into past times.

I am leading a group for a trekking company to climb Mount Elbrus. Located in the Caucasus Mountains at 18,442 ft Elbrus is technically the highest mountain in Europe, Mont Blanc is (15,782 ft).

This is a first for the company, but having led many trips for them, I have been offered this adventure. Of course I jumped at it without realising quite what I was letting myself in for.

We are a group of 27 people, and John Temple is my co leader, the idea being that we will divide into two groups once we arrive at the mountains. This is not workable. John is a widely experienced mountaineer and a member of the SMC, the prestigious Scottish Mountaineering Club. I am fortunate that he has agreed to come.

Having flown from England with TOMAR, the Rumanian airline, we were beginning to realise we were in for new experiences. During the flight someone had passed round a photocopied account of the Ascent of Mount Elbrus, *"technically easy, Alpine 'Facile'* the ascent is nevertheless serious. There is no shelter and high winds are common". Setting off at 2.45 a.m. the writer reports, *"as we ascended the final slopes of the East Summit we climbed into a strengthening wind. This became a gale at the top, forcing us to lie prone."* Sounds like Cairngorm. *"East and West ran the spine of the Caucasus, a thousand jagged peaks punctuated by the great icy triangles of the principal peaks"*...daunting stuff.

We look ahead and wonder. All is virgin territory and hard to foresee. No one here can tell us what it is like because no one has been there. Our minds reel, will there be crevasses, or storms, how will we deal with the altitude? Meantime we are taking two days to get there through Romania and Moldavia. I do not speak Russian.

Florin our 'local' guide seems unfamiliar with the station in Budapest, and we wander hither and thither looking for our train, amongst locals pouring forth from a train just drawn in. Old ladies wrapped in scarves clutching carrier bags, children boasting buckets and one man heaving a treadle sewing machine. All dressed generally in grey, brown and black. Surrounded by vast trains, we sit on our packs on the platform and eat our supper out of a polythene bag, fruit, and a slab of hamburger.

Finally Florin finds our train and we board. It is warm and we can smell the toilets. We have seats but no beds. So I climb into the luggage rack for the night.

Next day sees us at IASI, just on the border with Moldavia. Dawn finds us rolling past hills and towns with gothic windows and a stream of people going to work. A bus collects us from the train and we depart, whither we go and where we are, is all a mystery, but we go. Two hours later we are at the border. There is the usual bureaucratic hassle, flowers and flags and the clients take photographs. I take one and am arrested but due to intervention of our interpreter I am released. Too bad if the leader got taken off...

Three hours later and we are in Kishinev, a lush spot surrounded by vineyards, orchards and maize. Sergei Ginsberg meets us...smart in a fleece and Reeboks. He has come down from Moscow to escort us to the Baksan Valley in the Caucasus. He leads us into a grandiose restaurant, with woodcarvings, alcoves and *tromp l'oeil* ceilings. Last night's hamburger was a distant memory, so we wolf down spaghetti and goat before Sergei whisks us out and off to a small plane with 27 seats for 30, to fly to Nalchik, just north of the Caucasus Mountains.

Soon after a bus arrives and we make our way to the Baksan Valley, stopping en route to allow the bus driver to eat supper with his family before taking us to our hotel. This is an ex-Communist holiday hotel, built of marble and decorated with plants and boasting a vast television. Dinner is cheese, salami and profiteroles! The waitress brings them in on a delicate trolley more suited to flattering the Soviets.

The following are extracts from my trek diary:

September 3

The sun streams through the windows as I haul myself wearily out of bed. We go off on a familiarisation excursion up the Adul-Su Valley, a fresh green place punctuated by clumps of pines, with a glacial lake sunk into the moraine and goats everywhere. Our first lunch appears and we have tinned fish, cheese, bread, plums, eggs and beer. It rains so we crawl into one of the tin shelters (Priut) and I try to talk to Gima and Valery, who is the head of the mountain rescue team. It is all very different to home. In Russia what you cannot buy, or afford to buy, you make, so the guides working with us have stitched their own jackets, trousers, gaiters and rucksacks, and their hats and tops were hand knitted. They were engineers but as mountaineers who could not afford to go to the Caucasus and were earning about $50 a month, they took this job to enable them to be there and to supplement their meagre income. One or two were 'Masters of Sport', the result of having taken part in many climbing competitions, which used to be part of the climbing life under the Soviet regime.

Tonight John and I meet up with our Russian team to discuss the plans. We are 27 clients, with two leaders and the plan devised by the trekking company (far off in the office near London!) is to divide the group and work reasonably independently until we go to climb Mount Elbrus. We plan to explore some passes and work on fitness and acclimatization.

We are told all this is unworkable, and that the passes are thick with snow. Our whole dossier and itinerary for two weeks has just gone out of the proverbial window. At this stage I suspected that the guides did not want to do the passes, but as the trip had not been recce'd on the ground we could do nothing but accept! So it's back to the drawing board for a complete replanning of a trip in an area neither John nor I had ever visited. Each evening I would prepare the clients for the next replan of their trip.

September 4

Ice practice day. This is to be 'a perfect place for beginners' on a glacier locally. I was stupid and walked up the sides of the moraine in my plastic boots, which was a nightmare, they are rigid and unbending. Those who knew better walked in trainers and changed later. I divide the group into three, John and myself, with Boris and Sergei. Basic crampon practice and some use of ice axe.

As I help someone with their crampons I trip on my own straps and do a double somersault, badly damaging my knee. I turn round and there is Sergei descending a vertical ice wall with beginners! I put my group in a safe place to play, low ice walls, no rocks and no crevasses, and then saw people wandering off all over the place. It was like a Breughel illustration. Working with the unknown one assumes the safety rules will be the same as in the UK, they are not!

Suddenly a shout, Brian is on top of a serac, trips and falls twenty feet. He is lucky and is just bruised. I decide to call a halt to the day before anything worse happens, and we all go back to the hotel. We relax in the sauna. After the chill of the cold-water pool, we retire to another room for herb tea. The trouble is that the herbs are hallucinogenic, and we are high all evening!

September 5

A long day in store. I cannot walk, my knee has frozen, so I swallow large quantities of Brufen. I take a lift to the start of the walk. We are out today for eleven hours, ascending a grassy slope then clambering along a rock ridge. Stupendous views of mountains, Ushba and Schkhelda. My leg is sore but a quick dip in a freezing river sorts me out and I forget the pain. Everyone has enjoyed the day. Later on we have a party and dancing and tumblers of vodka, and the guides toast our forthcoming ascent.

September 6
Some folk have a go at rock climbing and some take off for a walk. I belay with a huge Russian Stichtplate. We meet up at the Green Hotel, a dirty hut in a dirty meadow and send out a search party for Brian who has decided to make his own route. Later we eat supper on the mud floor of the hut. We have macaroni and salami, and cheese sandwiches and tea. I sleep on a folding sunbed.

September 7
Alarm goes at 4 a.m. Hard-boiled eggs, cheese sandwiches and tea. The strong group go off to climb an unnamed point, and the rest stagger up the valley, and one lady falls in the river, so I take her back to main base. Everyone has enjoyed their day. Another party and more vodka. Tumblerfuls!

September 8
Breakfast today is spaghetti bolognaise followed by semolina! Then we explore the market at Cheget and people buy jerseys and hats, and postcards. We eat out...kebabs, pancakes full of meat and lots of wine. Another sauna at base (minus herb tea) and Sergei shows us slides of climbing in Russia. Peak Lenin. John and I remind the guides that WE are the people responsible for making this trip work, but with their help of course! (Do we think it's getting out of hand...?)

The Priut

September 9
Pouring rain and thick mist greet us at 7 a.m. We take the bus to the cable car and ascend to the shoulder of Elbrus where it is misty and cold. We explore, and go on up to the Red Barrels. These are old construction Nissan huts that give beds for climbers. Then we go higher to the main refuge, or Priut. Strange building looks like an upturned boat, the metal skin of the roof shines in the light. We have reached 13,635ft and everyone is happy to have managed this, and we run on down shouting and laughing. It is looking positive.

September 10

Up again to the Priut. This place is freezing, with no electricity and no heating. Water comes off the glacier behind the hut, and when it freezes at night snow is melted for water to drink. We walk up to Pastukhova Rocks, at 15,383ft they give essential guidance as to whether or not people are acclimatizing. It seems hard work, and not everyone makes it. Sergei gives us sliced sausage, cheese and tea and we find that this is supper. The views from here are beautiful, but we are hungry! The sinking sun glows red on the snow above us. Our cold bunks await us in the hut with no heat, just steel bunks in cold rooms, and no blankets. We rely on our sleeping bags and wear our clothes.

September 11

We are up at 3a.m., except for the eight who did not make it to the Rocks yesterday. We start with head torches then the starlight helps to guide us across the snow. Sergei, John and I are at the rear, and Boris and Valery out in front. Soon the strong group with Boris leave us behind and we stagger on, though some had to descend. At 17,500ft my legs give in and I stop in the col between the two tops. I am still living on Brufen. Fifteen people made it! I felt very flat but did go on to the summit twice in later years! This is the highest mountain in 'Europe'. We arrive back at three in the afternoon and Sergei rewards us with bread and cheese and spaghetti in milk! We crawl off to our cold beds.

View from shoulder of Mt Elbrus

September 12

We descend to the valley, but there is no petrol for the bus. Some people hitch, while some walk along the valley through Elbrus Town, a scatter of dirty tenements, haystacks, small houses, hens, rabbits and horses. There is one shop selling watermelons, a little bread and rotten apples.

After all of this we had some small walks until it was time to leave for home…little realising what this would entail.

Boris and Gima are driving to Moscow. They have about eight five-gallon tanks of fuel, which is not enough but they hope to pick some up. We have an uneventful return drive to Nalchik where we find no plane, and no pilot. Then when it comes we have to put 37 people on a 27-seater plane. John mutters something about air traffic regulations, and I say, "Just get on!" We lie in the aisle or stand in the tail holding on to a rail. We take off.

At Kishinev there is no bus to meet us. Someone wants food but I say that the first priority is to get to Bucharest for our flights and as we are late already we might have to forego a meal. "You don't give a ****if I eat or not, the job of a tour guide is to find food!" Sergei and I go to a takeaway and buy up all the pasties. Still no bus so we take the airport bus to the centre to try and find a train to Bucharest. It has gone but there is a local train to Ungeni, in Moldavia from where we hope to pick up a main line train from Moscow to Bucharest.

Sergei says, "It's difficult to have positive thinking now," and laughs, as he runs along the platform passing the tickets through a gap in the doors as the train pulls out; everyone has got on somewhere, I hope! Stuart buys bread from a woman on the train paying her in valuable US dollars. We are sitting on wooden seats, surrounded by locals with baskets of fruit, children and an old man with crutches.

Ungeni and it's 8.15 in the evening. We get out. I ask the group to stand and wait and head off to try and find out about trains and tickets. Women with plastic bags throng the hall, and when I say, "Bucharesti?" I am directed up the marble stairs to the Intourist office. There is a queue but I am ushered ahead to find six people in a huge room. I make it understood I need tickets to get to Bucharest for a plane…"How many?" She is horrified when I say 29 but then finds five first class sleepers, twelve second class and twelve seats…which she warned would be terrible, "there will be hundreds of people". I have to go and change money, and paid 29 US Dollars for all of us!

I ask for volunteers for the sitting places…and the young ones go for the sleepers. What a nightmare…I take the clients to the train to be told that they need to have their passports stamped before they can get on. When we finally get them on the train, they have to get into one train and walk through to one behind. They go. I return and the train pulls out, it turns out it hooks up behind the one we will be on later. The remainder of us go through Customs and then are locked in a room with no windows or air, 300 people waiting until the doors open at midnight when everyone rushes at the narrow door. I hang on to my bag as otherwise it would have been lost under the hundreds of feet. Out onto the platform, no idea where are going but I say "Bucharesti?" and hear *"da, da"* (yes, yes). We stand in the corridors, I hope everyone is on. We are jammed and cannot move. At last all the Romanians get off and we have some room, and I find that while I was trying to get tickets some of the clients had queued for an hour and managed to buy chicken, peppers, tomatoes and bread!

We are woken by a man asking for $40. I have no idea why, but give him $29 and when he gives me a kiss I know it is a bribe! How naive I am.

We finally get to Bucharest to find that our plane has gone. We meet our agent and I demand to be taken to the airport, but all other flights cost too much so I ask for a hotel for tonight and a tour of the town. Pompous flats with balustrades and columns, all of them empty. The Boulevard from the Royal Palace has a dual carriageway divided by fountains and flowers. Ceausescu had amazing visions of power. The average earnings are $40 a month and a diplomat we met on our plane said he earns $2 a day. Our hotel costs us $2 each.

Home to the UK. This has been some trip, was it really only fourteen days?

Moscow and off to the Pamirs, July 1992

The Registan, Samarkand

I was off to lead a trip across the Pamirs in the east of the Soviet land-mass and here I was arriving in Moscow at Sheremetyevo Airport. The first shock was to be asked for $5 to have my passport stamped. My introduction to bribes, so of course I said NO. But how exciting to be here at all.

I was staying in a flat on the outskirts of Moscow with two other leaders from Exodus Expeditions, for whom I was working. Apart from the fact our flat had three doors and three locks, and we were on the 11th floor of the fourth high-rise building, flat no 98, I didn't register much. Working with hard currency in Moscow was very dangerous, people had had their doors smashed open.

We went off into town to our agent, Alpindustria. Through Red Square and the Kremlin, and Lenin's tomb. I goggled at all this suddenly being in my life. St Basil's Cathedral, in Red Square, the famous little cathedral with all the domes. I visited McDonald's, which was the only place where I could find a toilet. Was accosted by a young lad anxious to practice his English, "Can I practice my English, it is as hard as finding a snowball in hell to speak it!" Dropped by in GUM's, a department store built in the 19th century to house 1,000 shops. *"It's worth visiting for the sparrow's eye view of the misery that is Soviet shopping". (Lonely Planet).* Now it houses Body Shop and Benetton, and some upmarket shops who accept hard currency, but only the wealthy have that.

Without thinking, I asked to be let off in Red Square on the way back. "See you!" I had a look around, then descended into the Metro station. Well! Fortunately having worked in Greece I had the basics of the Cyrillic alphabet, but spoke no Russian. Had not thought this through! I remembered the name of the station and by dint of saying this repeatedly, and hearing *"da, da"* (yes, yes) I made it down the marble halls to the correct platform. Wrought iron light fitments are strung with chandeliers in these cavernous marble spaces. I had to change trains, but somehow emerged at the end of the line to catch the no 707 to our flat. Emerged into daylight.

All is not over. I bought a bottle of champagne from a man sitting in a row of old people with upturned cardboard boxes in front of them, with vodka, beer, wine and herbs for sale. When I asked someone about the bus I was waiting for I found I was about to go the wrong way. When a bus turned up I enquired of the driver and got a volley of *"nyet"* (no). Fortunately someone on the bus spoke a little English and I explained that our flat was near the McDonald's factory. I had seen that and a Pizza Hut this morning as we left to go into town. One is a total idiot without the language.

I alighted from the bus but had a serious riddle still to solve. Which high rise flat was I in? After going up the wrong one, I wandered about in this vacant building site, and saw two *'babushkas'* (old women) on a bench. Then I remembered we were near a shop. *'Magazin'* in Russian, like the French, fortunately. So I asked these two if it was nearby. I found our high rise, and nearly fell in the door of no 98. Right one.

I could have been there still! Mountain travel is simpler.

Next day I met my group, did a tour of the Kremlin in the rain, and had a hamburger and fries in McDonald's, with an outsize photo of Big Ben on one wall. Next day we took our Aeroflot flight to Samarkand. For people new to Russian travel, it is a novelty to take off with people still putting things in overhead lockers. Lunch is a chicken leg in a plastic bag, and three buns.

We touch down three hours later. Samarkand.

Samarkand, '"The richest city of the East"….Intended capital of the world and certainly of Tamerlaine's Empire in the 13th Century. Invaded by Genghis Khan, and visited by Marco Polo, lived in by Omar Khyam and where the astronomer Ulugbek (grandson of Tamerlaine and ruler until 1449) invented astronomy, and set up a sextant in the 15th century. Prominent stopping point on the Silk Road.

Colour is everywhere. The Bazaar; Row upon row of spices, vegetables, peppers, onions, melons, almonds, peanuts, raisins, dried apricots, apples, cherries, grapes and barrows of flat bread……..what a land of plenty after Moscow. I watched fat-tailed sheep tended by shepherds in turbans, cloaks and heavy boots. Wonderful strong faces, ladies wearing vibrant coloured scarves, laughter exposing gold teeth, and Lurex thread sparkling in their brilliant shawls. There are trees everywhere and it all seems very affluent and very alive, bustling with customers. The air smells sour and dusty. Hot smells.

Tour of the Registan. These buildings are the centrepiece of Samarkand, an overload of towers and azure mosaics, once used as a school and a market place in the 15th century. Coming from the west it is odd to just wander about something so magnificent, ornate and special with no tourist emphasis at all.

But we are here to walk across the Pamirs, a large mountain mass lying east of the Caspian Sea, in Kyrgyzstan, on the Chinese border. To reach the start we board a bus and travel for nine hours, then transfer to an old truck. Faced with a river crossing, we watch as a young lad rides his motorbike into the torrent, where waist deep he swamps to a stop. Our truck bounces through.

The country is magnificent. Bare rock peaks soar skyward all around into a deep azure sky. One huge snow spire blocks the end of the valley. The lower slopes are full of juniper and flowers, and we pass some Kirghiz nomads who feed us Aryan (Yoghourt). They keep sheep, goats, cows and turkeys!

Our base camp is at 8000ft we think, but no one is sure. Our large Russian crew welcome us into camp that night with a party in the tent (silk, made out of old parachutes! Russians are masters of ingenuity. What they need they make). We drink champagne, and try the local treat, which is sour pig fat, and garlic, washed down with vodka. It is reserved for special people like leaders!

Valery had rigged up a shower. Water from the stream ran through a pipe, which entered a double skinned pipe, which was heated by a blow torch at each end. At one point one end exploded. But the brave had great showers inside a polythene sheeted tent.

Beautiful walks here, amidst flowers, rushing water and herds of magnificent horses roaming wild. Iskander, Aleksander, and Aksu, towering giants of rock. Washing in the streams, relaxing and preparing to cross the 14,000ft Aktubek Pass into the Ort Chasma valley. Two people get sick, one person goes down with altitude sickness and one man suffers sunstroke. Not looking good! I am worried at leaving them here for three days with two guides, to do some walks to help them acclimatise and get better, before flying them in by helicopter to our camp at 14,000ft...as it is a plateau there with no way to descend lower.

We cross the pass. It's a long haul up and Volodia my guide has no idea of leadership. Carrying an 80lb load he heads vertically up the scree. No one can follow, so the group is spread higgledy piggeldy over the slope, staggering breathlessly, at the start of a nine hour day. After seven hours we reach the top of the Pass. Lying there on the sand, with a large rock buttress and a hanging glacier above, I feel in touch with the earth, healed from worries. Three hours later we reach our *Kosh* (shepherd's hut) where we are to camp. The shepherd calms his dogs.

No porters and no horses. (The horses had had to take an easier, if longer, route round) No food. Volodia seems to have forgotten that he is carrying the soup and dehydrated food I gave him. I locate the shepherd who lets me have some dry crusts and cold goat for the group, and negotiate to use the *Kosh* for the group to sleep. The *Kosh* has half a roof! Between us we have four sleeping mats, four sleeping bags and one tent for Malcolm who is allergic to dog hairs! Volodia doesn't seem to care about us or our gear. I climb up a little and light a bonfire to guide the porters in with our bags. At midnight we are still three sleeping bags short so I borrow from the Russians. Just as I am lying down I mutter to myself, "I wonder what tomorrow will throw at me". A voice outside says "MA, Paul has been kicked by a horse, and is working himself into a state about being stuck here alone, waiting for a helicopter". I offer some medication and reassurance and collapse in my bag.

A whole new day. The horses arrived in the night. Natasha is warming last night's soup in the Kosh, the sheep are hanging their heads against the river bank. Cooling off in the shade. We are alone here. Some very perilous river crossings on wet logs, holding Valery's hand, and then we can stroll through woods and climb to Kosh Mainock, our next camp. Here we have to crush the grass and flowers to flatten the tent floor. An idyllic spot, with the next pass just two hours above us.

Karavshin, the climbers' camp, and there are two men here from Edinburgh! Pyramid Peak, white against the blue, and the amphitheatre of Asan Usan, granite spires steep and sheer reminding me of the mountains in Patagonia, or Yosemite. Here we have a minor epic, when two of the group decide, against my advice, to cross the rushing river. One slips off the log and hangs onto a rope. Aghast and unable to do anything I pray he holds on till Sergei reaches him. He does and so escapes a nasty swim in white water and boulders.

We are out of bread so I organise pancakes. We have these with honey out of a plastic bag. Food here is almost adequate. Breakfast is porridge or kasha, made with wheat, barley or rice. After this there is dry bread and tea. No milk. Lunch is dry bread and a slice of salami or cheese and an ancient apple. Suppers are invariably cabbage soup with

Group amongst the magnificent Pamirs

tinned meat, followed by mashed potato, or rice with tinned meat. Vegetarians eat the same without the meat.

Despite uncertainty, our first helicopter arrives today. We were told we must decamp and pack and wait. If the helicopter does not come, we re-erect our tents and do the same next day! Our five friends, fit and acclimatised, arrive in it. We have ten minutes to load, as the helicopter cannot stay long at this altitude. A large mess tent belonging to a Russian group is flattened by the onrush of wind, and in scrambling aboard I recall seeing heads pushing up against the fabric, as breakfast disturbed, they try to get out. It is funny to see. Our pilots are good. Very good. We fly for about a hundred miles, skimming over passes, dusting the snow off summits. Sometimes the blades seem barely to miss the rock.

We land. We throw everything out onto the dust. The helicopter leaves, and in a cloud of dust we lie on our baggage to stop it blowing away. A huge noisy bird.

Where are we? On both sides the hills rise, steep, unclimbable shale. Is this a mistake, are we deposited in the wrong place? I think so! A muddy black torrent rages down the valley, a deep rumble from moving rocks below. No way to cross it, or to leave the valley. So tomorrow's walk will be upstream and next day downstream, and I hope the helicopter comes back on day three. Life goes on and Natasha bakes more pancakes, this time putting the inedible grey fish inside, so pleasurable anticipation turns to disgust! I congratulate her on the effort! (Our staff, as well as being mountain men and women, are usually engineers!)

Ruth makes a patio outside the entrance to her tent to keep out the sand. Here the colours are of sand and stone, reds, blacks and greys. Strange upthrusted strata, vertical stripes. We pound rocks to isolate the cubes of iron pyrites. Spiny shrubs in the sand and a snow leopard's paw print.

Lake camp near Chinese border

Supper in our silken bell tent sitting on huge stones round a stone table the lads have made. We sit on rocks, one each. Tonight we have a treat. Pasta and Sarah's tomato and onion sauce, and I make chocolate mousse which I put in the plastic boxes from the medical kit.

Next day the helicopter comes and we all pile in and fly over another pass in a snowstorm. Our last campsite is near Lake Karakul. We can see China. All is not over for us yet. A late afternoon katabatic wind threatens to flatten camp. Spend an hour and a half piling rocks on the flysheets but in the end the tents caved in during the night.

Our campsite is far from the Lake, but Volodia says we can cross the river. It is a mile across! Next morning we try. It is very cold. I get very cold feet and return to thaw them out. Sitting on the bank, rubbing them, I am crying with the pain. It takes two hours. I stay in my tent. A day off! We will wait for the truck.

Next day the promised truck does not appear, but did we think it would! We walk out and find a bus waiting on the desert sand. The driver says he thinks our Moscow flights are being cancelled, so we have a large lunch, on new food, gorging ourselves on bread, cheese, cabbage soup and melon. And vodka! I decide we must get to Osh to make sure of our flights, so we drive for six hours past yurts and yak farms, camels and dull prefabricated houses in villages with trees!

We camp amongst trucks and old caravans in Osh. We have secured our flights, and have a party. Valery is given a radio and Anatoly wants my ski sticks. But there are more treks for me.

We board our plane for Moscow, I fall asleep and wake to find a tray of cold stew and dry bread. Eat nothing. The plane lands twice on the way to Moscow, to refuel, and so takes seven hours. We wait two hours for our bags, then off to my hotel where I sort rooms for clients… It is 5 a.m. Pete Burrell (of Exodus) gives me a chicken sandwich and my mail from home, which is wonderful!

Then I am off to the airport to fly south to Mineralnye Vody where I pick up a group to climb Mount Elbrus! Hear of Campbell's group in Georgia being woken by bandits with guns who took sleeping bags and watches. We are now abandoning Georgia as a trekking area. Thank Goodness! A taxi for 3 hours and I stumble into the Hotel Itkol to meet the group and excuse myself and go to bed!

Mani Rimdu Festival Nepal, snowbound, 1995

My son, Peter, was down in the Antarctic with British Antarctic Survey. This is my Fax to him:

> *'Just to let you know that I am alive and well, and home again. I wrote you a letter while I was wandering around Nepal, raised a mug of tea to you on your birthday, the day of the Mani Rimdu Dance, and the snow storm which changed the course of our trip. Pretty mega really – big landslide killed 25 in Gokyo Valley where we would have been if the Mani Rimdu had not been delayed three days to suit the moon... People killed all over the place, with frostbite. 1000 yaks snuffed it, suffocated in the snow. Porters died of hypothermia. Still had people who thought it was all MY fault, or Himalayan Kingdom's fault that we couldn't do our planned itinerary. Nice to be home...'*

The *Mani Rimdu* Festival is held twice a year, once in about June, at Thame, and again six months later at Tengboche, a large monastery in the Khumbu, near Mount Everest. It takes place straight after the full moon in October and is tied in with the Tibetan Lunar Calendar. It is a famous event, and the Masked Dance, a culmination of many days of ceremonies and meditation, is open to the public. This is the day that the *Rinpoche* ('precious one' the title given to the head of a monastery) blesses the public and is an opportunity for Tibetan and Sherpa communities to gather and celebrate with the monastic community.

We were trying a trip to walk into the famous Gokyo area with further exploration to Lobuche and perhaps Kala Pattar, to let people have a closer look at Mt Everest.

After the usual walk in to Namche Bazaar we prepared to arrive in Tengboche for the Mani Rimdu, but found out that due to the phase of the moon the festival would be delayed three days. This meant we had to reschedule our trip, as we had intended to attend the festival and then visit Gokyo before going on up to Lobuche. Initially this was a bit annoying, but we made a side trip to Pangboche and then returned.

How fortunate this turned out to be! Had we gone into Gokyo as planned we might have been caught in the avalanche that swooped down on the lodge at Phanka, en route to Gokyo, killing 26 people.

Flags outside Tengboche Monastery

Yellow hats

But we were still at Tengboche and the snow had not begun. We enjoyed the Mani Rimdu Festival enormously. This festival is so special, as it includes old and young, Sherpas and Tibetans and trekkers, everyone participates and there is fun and laughter. It was wonderful to be part of it, all crunched together on the perimeter of the courtyard. We had enjoyed the spectacle of the monks dancing with their large masks, and the clown calling in a trekker for a fun game with a stick and humorous attacks. We had watched the monks of the Gelukpa Sect, wearing their big yellow hats entering the central square of the monastery, and heard the horns being blown outside in the wide open area overlooked by the high mountains, Kantega and Tamserku, then we had partaken in the throwing of rice.

That night, the snow fell, in buckets full. I watched as the tent sides began to droop under the weight, then at 5 a.m. I got up. I went round the tents, trying to shake the snow off their sagging walls but it was too much. The kitchen tent had flattened. I told everyone to clear their tents, bringing some stuff, and managed to find room for us all in a crowded lodge nearby. What to do?

Snow flattens tents overnight

Gradually horrifying stories filtered in, of porters found dead on the passes leading out from Mera Peak and higher up, of trekkers trapped in Chukkung and Gokyo and of yaks suffocating in the deep snow, a thousand yaks succumbed.

Then the sky began to be filled with helicopters and we heard of people being airlifted out, although it took many planes as many people were stuck. We did hear of people trying to buy their way to a place on a chopper. Some people told of crawling on the snow to try to get out. It was too deep to walk.

Meanwhile, I was left with the problem of what to do with the clients, for the rest of their trip. There were disgruntled comments, "I have saved up for three years for this trip, and I want to go up to Lobuche to see Everest".

"You are scared of the snow, M.A."

I held a 'pow wow' in the mess tent with the clients, and told them why we could not now go to Gokyo, or Lobuche. Much moaning from three of them, then later a swig of whisky from a client along with, "You need this M.A. That was very difficult for you, you did well".

So I arranged for the disgruntled three to go up Pheriche, for a night, as that was as far as they could get and is still almost a normal day's walk from Lobuche, in usual weather. Sorted out Sherpas. Then took some of them on a short day walk, so that we also got to Pheriche for lunch, then walked back, the snow up to our thighs. The three were not impressed, obviously thinking that if it was that easy they could have gone higher! There was nowhere else to go. Most people were making their way down to Lukla and out.

Escaping through
deep snow

It was a very scary trip, and I was relieved in Namche Bazaar to meet people I knew who had finally made it out of the mountains and were safe. But many people had died. The newspaper headlines read, *'Avalanche toll reaches 63, and 549 people airlifted to safety.'*

When I reached home in Aviemore, Himalayan Kingdoms sent me the copy of a letter from the three, complaining vigorously that I had ruined their dream holiday by not taking them where they intended to go, and that, 'M.A. does not like snow'. I was staunchly supported by Steve Berry, the head of Himalayan Kingdoms.

Dolpo and West Nepal, nearly avalanched, 1996

Breakfast at camp Dho Tarap

'RESCUERS find bodies of US couple who died while climbing Himalayas

Rescuers dug through eight feet of snow yesterday to uncover the bodies of a US medical school dean, his wife and three Nepalese who died while sleeping in their tent in the Himalayas.' (Newspaper 11 Nov, 1996. Kathmandu, Nepal)

The group was last seen on 21 October near Shey Gompa. The helicopter pilot who flew their bodies out to Dunai, said, "They were all inside the same tent. It seems all of them died in their sleep. They were all in their sleeping bags with no shoes on and lying in a row".

It is *probable* that the deep snow submerged their tent and they all suffocated, it is usual to knock the snow off all night when this occurs.

Dolpo only opened to visitors in 1988 and has been wildly acclaimed as one of Nepal's best trekking regions. As an area it became known after the publication of Peter Matthieson's journey, made famous in his book, *'The Snow Leopard'*. This was Peter Matthieson's spiritual journey in quest of self, as he suffered from the loss of his wife from cancer in America the previous year. Also David Snelgrove who discovered it in 1956 and wrote a book *'Himalayan Pilgrimage'* about his seven months in west and central Nepal increased interest in the region.

The area of Dolpo, in the Jumla District of Nepal, lies 224 miles west of Kathmandu. Nepalganj is in the Terai, the south of Nepal, and is wonderfully rural and hot. Wooden wheels and farms. Eventually we flew to Juphal in a twin Otter and could start our trek.

Our aim was to head north to Dho Tarap, a Tibetan style village on a wide valley, which used to be an important trading post, for people from the north, Tibet, and the south, east and west. Thereafter we would cross two passes and end up at Phoksundo Lake, before trying the last pass, the Kagmara La, and head out to Jumla.

Two of my clients, Albert Chapman and Raymond Fawcett, have kindly lent me their diaries. I have chosen to lead into this momentous trip with quotes from Albert's diary from which I have permission to quote in part. Raymond's diary takes up the account of the dramatic crossing between the Numa la and the Baga la. Both men have such observant eyes and write so vividly that they are able give a better, fresh record of the journey as clients, than I could as a leader, whilst my mind was almost immediately totally filled with problems to solve.

For this trip leads forward, in steps, until the climax in the mountains, and the anticlimactic but relaxed walk out at the end. Thankful to have made it!

"Day 4
Flight from Kathmandu at 3.20. Magical flight through southern foot-hills, forests, rivers, clouds and squally rain. Indian girl with baby boy sat next to me. Vivid green of paddy fields. Flew at ridge height. Landed in grassy field to let off a Nepalese Minister in rain. On to Nepalganj and Chinese meal in the Sneha Hotel.

Day 5
Woke at 4.15 a.m. Eggs for breakfast. Today's flight cancelled due to the bad weather in the hills, so we took horse drawn carts (with wooden wheels) on a tour. Our guide proudly took us to the 'hospital'. It was difficult for us to walk down the corridors past people lying on

stretchers, or on the floor, on filthy much used sheets and blankets, being fed by relations, to share his pride in this place."

But for them to have a hospital at all was a huge bonus. In the south of Nepal, the heat delivers smells, loads of them…hot smells, curry smells, smells of cow dung, or foetid water. All hang low in the dusty air. There are many people, women in old cotton saris, cradling a child on a hip, but always an earring and bracelets. Men are hammering at pots, or sitting under a tree, as men do, watching the busy world go by. It is hot here, and people are reluctant to hurry, music blares from a radio lying behind some planks of wood in the sawdust.

Albert continues:

"Day 6
4.30 a.m. call again and back to airport and this time we flew. Over foothills of increasing height, 45 mins, to land on a runway which was very short, and rough and dipped in the middle. Exciting landing. (The guidebook says it is one of the more dodgy and difficult places to fly into in Nepal!) Walked on down to the Beri Khola (river) and on to Dunai. Campsite in the hotel grounds. Pines, walnuts and juniper.

Days 7 and 8
Delightful walk by river, surrounded by sweet corn and millet at camp. Met two French girls walking in. Warm sun and paths through flowers, herbs and marijuana. Tall trees. Crossed a long suspension bridge and into Tarap Khola valley. Very narrow, amazing paths built into side of the cliffs. Began to rain heavily and continued all the way to camp. Conscious that this is snow higher up. Where we hope to go.

Days 9 and 10
Didn't sleep too well. Cloudy, no sun, and occasional light rain. Arrived at Bhedi Kharka before porters who had a horrid time crossing muddy col. Bridges are very dodgy. Stopped for lunch in a cave, and the rain turned to sleet. Porters refused to go on to planned Kharka (camp spot) and we camped half an hour short. Spent two hours in a cave watching it snow, with Sherpas on one side and porters on the other! Impasse. Then into tents covered in snow and damp inside. Sherpas continually banging sides of tent to shake snow off. Porters in a cave."

This was not a happy time to be a leader (I sometimes wonder, is it ever?) As we stayed in this dark damp spot, various people who had gone higher came past us, going 'out', retreating. An American party who had gone higher came through and said snow was knee deep in Dho Tarap. A herd of twenty yaks and three ponies, together with a Tibetan Yak herder family, passed us, also going lower. For my S*irdar*, Sonam, and me this was desperate. I hoped to get the clients at least to Dho Tarap and thought that, even if the snow was hard for us, if everyone got there and we had to retreat, at least they could feel they had achieved some part of what they came for.

Next day I discovered that one of the clients was suffering from altitude sickness and had to descend, Jenny and Mike departed, with the only Sherpa I could afford to give them, knowing what might be ahead, a young lad new to the job, but I felt this couple would manage, and the country was easier lower down. They would join us at Phoksundo Lake later if they felt well enough. The two French girls we met earlier, were also going down.

Readers may wonder why I persevered to go on up, when the whole world was going down. Because I know how clients feel, they have spent a lot of money on a trip, and want to try every possible option to see it through. A lot of time and planning has also gone into bringing them here. I always did my best, though sometimes had to say "No" very firmly. But I had the safety of the whole group at stake, not just the clients, also the porters and the staff…and myself!

A clear sunny morning provided respite, and the day looked inviting. I decided to go. Our walk up was stunning. White snowy mountains surrounded us, there were sheer rich brown cliffs and gorges and lots of birds by the river. It seemed the birds were rejoicing in a break in the weather. Writing now, 18 years later, I now find it amazing that I did continue to lead the trip up against a steady tide of people going the other way.

Dho Tarap stands in an open valley, at 13,254ft, it has the highest barley fields in the world, we were told, though I do wonder about Tibet itself, which mostly lies at 13,000ft. We felt very privileged to be in this place.

Dho Tarap has Tibetan style houses with flat roofs, and the people here are both Bon Po and Bhuddist. The women wear *chubas* home

House Dho Tarap

spun clothing that is sometimes dyed maroon and they favour fabric Tibetan style boots with upturned toes. Indeed when the Dalai Lama fled Tibet many of the Kampas (the nomads from Amdo and east Tibet) came here, to escape the Chinese.

Albert notes that it was, *"beautiful weather, though freezing overnight. There is a quarter moon, and stars are stunning. Up before bed tea and drank it on other side of the river in the sun. Dried my washing of three days ago, also sleeping bag and mat. Explored side valley to Kakar Gompa".*

We visited one of the flat roofed houses, the firewood, gathered from far off, where there is wood, is piled on the roof, and the inner courtyard has a ladder, a shaft of wood, with steps cut into it, bucket fashion, to take you on the roof. The family live in a room off the court-yard where the woman of the house has a small fire in the middle of the floor. Round about are shelves with metal or plastic jugs and bowls. She was cooking potatoes, which have become a staple in Nepal, and she handed us one and also mashed one up for the baby. Not much you might think, a potato? But each potato is a valuable treasure, as crops here at 13,000ft have a very short growing season, with snow lying well into June. The ground is also poor and stony, and is rock hard for months. Later I was to trek in Zanskar, and found that there the local people will take some soil indoors during the winter to keep it unfrozen and then lay this soil on top of the snow. This soil is then sown with seeds as the snow below it gradually melts the soil simultaneously waters the seeds.

We met two girls carrying a baby. The girls were shy, and only came near us as they felt brave, as a pair. One of them combed her hair with twigs, and it was lovely to see how they answered what they saw as a need without a plastic comb.

I was enjoying a day of seeming freedom, exploring this magical place, while of course wondering about the Numa La and the Baga La, the two passes ahead of us. Unknown to me Sonam had sent a Sherpa up to the next village to find out if the passes were open. On our small walk, we looked at the pass through binoculars and it did seem very white and I assumed it would be impassable. But Ang Karma returned and told us yaks had crossed, so it was open. I was devastated, as I was not at all sure about it…I had little information to go on, but, well, if it was open…? Clients excited. "Great, we can go!"

Girls from village of Dho Tarap

Next day we ventured further up the valley, and actually met a British-Norwegian lady, who had seen a snow leopard near here a few weeks ago, all we see are tracks. We distracted ourselves from the future by visiting the Crystal Mountain School, which was a real delight. Lots of wee children in maroon *chubas*. The children come from all around, and have a dormitory there. The school motto is, 'The aim of education is not knowledge but action.' Perhaps a good title for a debate.

Okay, if we are going to do this, it needs a good structure. I got the clients and trek staff together at Tok-Kyu and gave them a stern briefing on the morrow. I said we would get up at 2 a.m., to have time. I said it was imperative the porters stayed near the group, as they were carrying the sleeping bags and tents, and in case of emergency, we needed these close to hand.

The day did not exactly 'dawn' but we rose at 2 a.m. and were off at 4.30 a.m. It was a hard slog up, with thick snow, three feet deep. The Sherpas broke trail, and we followed. I was accompanying Ron, a dear man who wore a catheter, so we got further and further behind, as he was, of course, very slow. I was left behind with him and one Sherpa, and the group had disappeared out of sight. When Ron and I arrived at the col and found the group sunning themselves, they said: "Where have you been M.A.? We have been here for hours", I lost my temper completely, as it was very dangerous for us to be left alone in these conditions, deep snow and at 17,500ft. I asked them to stay closer for the descent into camp. They took off. Ron and I were on our own with two Sherpas as it got dark, walking along a path, on now freezing snow, above a river.

I had two torches, the Sherpas had two sleeping bags and that was all we had if we had to 'dig in'. No sign of group, and no idea how far to go. Finally a light shone ahead, and Sonam had come to look for us. We followed him to the mess tent, it was 8.30 p.m., and we had been on the go for 16 hours. When I got there I found everyone in the tent drinking tea, no tents up. The team were totally done in. I lost my temper again, and went out to stamp down the snow for the tents. We ate in the cook tent. Well done, Pasang the cook.

Before retiring, Sonam and I discussed the following day, the Baga La. The next pass is 17,000ft. But to stay where we were, despite everyone being exhausted, seemed to me to be a very dangerous option as there was no way out from there except over the two passes. Sonam agreed.

Frozen boots and exhaustion delayed our departure until about 10.30 a.m. I made cardboard sides for the porters' goggles, to try to cut out the sun. We started up. I took one look ahead at the classic avalanche slope we had to cross, facing the sun, and wanted to go vertically down and up the other side. But no one was having it. Meantime some of the porters were crying, the sun was causing snow blindness. But what to do? We had to go. I allowed the Sherpas and porters to cross the slope first, and then, hoping it had passed the test, we went.

Once over we descended (with some relief) about 1,000ft, to sloping ground where we erected the tents. The party was severely exhausted and some had dreadfully swollen and cracked lips. One porter was almost blinded and had to be led.

But, we were out!

Raymond's graphic account of that perilous crossing follows:

"1996 Tuesday 10 October, between the Numa la and the Baga la
I am writing this in my sleeping bag. The tent is pitched on two feet of snow, the ice on my rucksack inside the tent is rock hard. I led my small convoy into camp at 8.10 yesterday evening, the last two hours in

darkness, having got up at 2 a.m. yesterday morning. It was a long, hard, worrying and exhausting day.

Our early breakfast yesterday was somewhat thwarted by the porters' inability to get sorted out. We had planned to be away at 3 a.m. but did not start walking till 4.30 a.m. M.A.'s instructions that the group keep together were quickly ignored as Pete sped off, followed by Shirley, while Ron was painfully slow, exacerbated by a painful gut and many toilet stops (catheter). From the outside the day had the makings of a disaster, which it very nearly became.

The going was very cold to start with, over uneven ground but with minimal height gain. Dawn came soon after we started climbing but real warmth came an hour or two later.

For the first couple of hours I stayed with Ron and M.A. Pasang Yellow Socks was with us too and carried Ron's bag. M.A. became concerned that Ron might not make it to the pass and would therefore need his kit bag and a tent to be taken back down with him. Pasang and I went off at greater speed to get word to Sonam and the main group. Some of the group came into sight. I shouted at them to wait but the buggers just looked at me and carried on.

Sonam went back to see M.A. Marion, who had been at the back, left me to recuperate and joined the others. She asked them to hang on so we could all regroup with M.A. but they were off.

The climb was exhausting under a roasting sun. The lip salve in my pocket melted, the chocolate bar did the same, and the jelly babies coalesced. I had to ration my water. The thin air near the top made me adopt a walking regime of 40 steps (I counted) followed by rest. I reached the pass 17,500ft at 11.30 a.m. after seven hours walking. Pete had been there since 10. M.A. arrived at 1.30 with an exhausted Ron. As a cold wind had got up we could not linger, and poor Ron had only ten minutes before starting down. The wind had started up and it was cold.

My water was gone now, and I took to eating snow. I watched three ravens and wondered at their relationship. The Sherpas made a cup of warm tea for us.

The path to the camp, on snow, was far further than any of us had expected. As before, some of the group sped ahead. I stayed with M.A. and Ron till it was agreed Sonam (as head Sherpa) and I should go ahead, to sort out camp and group.

After a river crossing we were dismayed to see the path climbing again. By now it was coming up to 6 pm and getting dark. Marion had the idea of marking M.A.'s way in the snow with her stick.

The path became dangerous contouring round a snow slope, where to slip would mean probable death and certain severe injury. We picked up a French couple who had turned back...and I found myself leading three frightened people over awful ground. Then we met one of the porters, a very young lad who had simply stopped in fear because he could not see his way on the steep snow slope. He stayed with us, walking in front of me while I lit his path.

We met Sonam out looking for M.A. We were glad to see him. By now the slope had lessened, no longer dangerous, but it had been a frightening hour or more. At one point Marion lost her grip on her pole, which rushed several hundred feet down the hard snow slope to the river below.

Shortly after our arrival at the tent we heard a whistle, apparently blown in distress. I put on some warm clothes and, unable to find anyone else to leave the warm tent, I went a bit up the path and met M.A. She was glad to see my light but generally angry at the way the day had gone. The whistle had not been hers. Maybe someone died out there that night.

I was quite finished and managed to spill my soup down my trousers. We had been on the go for twenty hours.

We ate in the cook tent and then retired to our tents. I was on my own and the temperature was minus 10C in the morning, at 8 a.m., and no doubt lower during the night. In the morning our boots were frozen solid and we could not put them on.

The news just in is that we are going to try to get out of here tomorrow and camp at the Baga La high camp. This camp is 14,763ft. Baga La is 16,502ft.

Wed 11 October

Amazingly the Sherpas brought tea to our tents and even washing water!

Sonam, Ankame and one other Sherpa set off before us to do the exhausting work of trail breaking. The rest of us set off at about 10.30 a.m. The first part was very steep so we were all slow. Eventually we were in sight of the lead Sherpas who seemed to have hit a particularly difficult patch.

We watched the Sherpas painful progress and I decided to try to reach them and take a turn to relieve them. I floundered about in the snow, which, though partly compacted, gave way frequently. Then we watched in alarm as the Sherpas cut across a steep snowfield with a high risk of avalanche. (M.A. was holding the group back till she saw what happened). We had considered what we would have done had we failed to reach the pass by nightfall. We would have to have camped high up and continued next day. Not a great option.

The Sherpas seemed to be getting away with their risky venture so we all followed. It was quite frightening as a fall would have been difficult to stop.

We made it over. We were fed in our tents...rice and dal...but no one really cared, and somehow...well, we are over the worst now.

Thurs 12 October

06.40 in the morning and although the sun has been up for nearly an hour it has not reached our camp. It is desperately cold. Like the previous night our tents are pitched on snow, but unlike that time, they are also on a slope. Last night seemed to go on forever. The tissues I used in the night are frozen solid.

The hard crossing has taken its toll. Ron, Shirley and Albert all have terribly swollen and cracked lips and wracking coughs, verging on bronchitis. Pete has damaged his Achilles tendon and is finding the walking agonising. M.A.'s cold still bad. I have a bit of a cough and a sore nose from both blowing it and having too much sun on it. I seem to be the fittest.

We got away about 10.40 a.m. and finally left the snow at about 12.15 and started down a lovely flat meadow. It is so great go be off snow. It is like coming back to life from the land of death.

The good news is that we are over the Baga La and on our way to Ringmo and safety. It was not until late yesterday that I thought we would make it out of the bad place between the passes.

Yesterday's walk would have been a stroll under normal conditions. We tackled it in several feet of new snow. No one has been over the pass since the storm.

Descending after the passes

Our camp resembles a TB ward. Everyone, trekkers, Sherpas, porter, are coughing their guts out. There is fairly heavy frost outside."

I take up the story again:

The next day we faced the same scenario with frozen boots and we got away about 11 a.m.

We crossed a lot of snow and avalanche debris and made it into a superb, soft Alpine valley with pine trees, and grass, and flowers and finally to Ringmo and Phoksundo Lake, where we found Mike, but Jenny had flown home.

Next day we submitted to paradise. A deep blue, turquoise lake was surrounded by trees, pines and something like a birch. We washed our clothes, aired the sodden, dirty tents and Albert went off past the chortens to visit Ringmo monastery, where he found four cheerful monks, mending the roof. Albert wrote: "had a bad night, lips swollen, bad cough like everyone else, but also on chest, nose bleed. I look like Yasser Arafat. Felt very weak". He was

Phoksundo lake

given some homeopathic pills for his lips by a German doctor.

Unbelievably two clients were still giving me a hard time, after all we have escaped they now want to do the Kagmara La, the last pass. I am incredulous and unmoving. "It's what it says in the itinerary". No chance.

We decided on an alternative low-level route to Jumla, and left this wonderful place with the autumn oranges and browns contrasting stunningly with the blue lake. (Even now the same two clients were angry we were not going straight to Juphal and on to Kathmandu for a few extra days there, it was Albert who insisted we go to Jumla). We saw white and blue gentians. It is from here that one would take the left hand side of the lake and a track that leads north to Shey Gompa. We met a yak man who told us the Kagmara La might be open. But I am not interested. We have made it to here and are lucky indeed. Enough is enough. Not just the clients in their duvet jackets and heavy boots and thick gloves, but the much less substantially clothed and shod trek crew and porters, have suffered hugely for us, and I was not putting them through any more.

On the way out we met a group who had been turned back at the Kagmara La, one lot whose porters got frostbite and snow blindness.

I think we started to enjoy the relief of just walking along a track. The trees seemed rich in their colour and softness, pines, walnut and evergreen oak, after the barren snow and cold. Birds chattered. Goats scattered in villages and horses grazed in fields. Albert was shaved by Mike and Peter, and bought some apples. We killed and ate a lame lamb the crew had bought on the way, and on the Maura La we met two postmen, one from Kaigaon and one from Jumla, swapping post! We camped in a clearing in the forest and were warned to keep the zips down on our tents as there were snakes about! Albert notes his bronchitis is clearing and his lips are healing! We laugh with one another and exchange jokes.

What a trip. We got into Jumla and everyone felt a bit anticlimactic. It had been a totally exhausting, demanding and rather dangerous trip, but we had come through. It was well above the remit of any 'trek' although the description was 'strenuous'. After some Rara noodles at the airport in Jumla we flew to Kathmandu. I don't recall a party here. Maybe we were just too tired, gave the tips, said thank you and left.

Trip over. People departed to Pilgrim's Book Shop, or to sample the culinary delights of KCs. I did the accounts and the Leader's report. Flew home to a welcome party and, "Did you have a good holiday?"

And then we read of the folk who died, in the same blizzard that hit the mountains where we were. At the same time.

M.A. and Angus on safe return

The Kora round Mount Kailash, Tibet, 1998

Mt Kailash

Kailash and Lake Manasarovar are, according to *Lonely Planet*, two of the most remote travel destinations in the world. The four main rivers of India, the Ganges, Sutlej, Brahmaputra and Indus all rise near to Mount Kailash. Within less than a hundred miles of Kailash are the headwaters of the Indus, the Tsangpo, the Sutlej and the Karnali. The Tsangpo flows east and becomes the Brahmaputra, the Karnali joins the Ganges, the Indus flows northwest into Ladakh, the Sutlej makes its way southwest through Spiti, into north India. I was fortunate to lead a trip to this astonishing region for Mountain Kingdoms in 1998. This account consists of extracts from diaries kept by myself and John, one of the trek members.

Dramatis personae

I do think it is important to give a brief summary of those on this trip:

John, who had travelled extensively and explored many parts of the world, including Patagonia, on his own, had retired from the Ordnance Survey. He has kindly given me permission to use some of his

129

wonderfully detailed and evocative notes in this chapter. He carried balloons, which he distributed to all the children we met on the trip, though I think some mothers did wonder what they might be!

Roger came from Bristol and was a lawyer for Mountain Kingdoms. He had travelled overland from London to Moscow to Lhasa before turning up, dressed in a *shalwar kameez,* to meet me in the dining room of the Summit Hotel in Kathmandu. He was not at all what I expected the company lawyer to be like but he was wonderful company, and along with John was a huge source of moral support. I enjoyed his sense of humour and his *beedees,* Indian roll up cigarettes!

Susan was 28, from Ireland and had an obvious limp, which we noticed in the departure lounge at Heathrow. It turned out she had had cerebral palsy as a child, and has trouble with walking as well as balancing. She cannot carry her own pack, and cannot do up her shoelaces or pack her bag...

Two Canadians, whom I will call J and H...who were on a personal mission, namely to bury J's second husband's ashes on the *Kora.* H very slow, and J very determined. Both had done many exciting things in their lives, and J was an avid photographer and writer and very fit, with stacks and stacks of gear, which proved to be a rather selfish problem for the group. J knew her 'rights' as a paying client!

Then there are four Sherpas. Karma Lama is our *sirdar.* Our Liaison Officer is Indira Yogi ('Deputy Dawg') a policeman from Simikot. He tries hard but his English is confusing and his facts are frequently quite wrong. He claims to have climbed Everest, but we wonder. Then we have Pasang, our cook, Ang Geelo and Goan, who put up our tents.

Kailash itself, *"Has been variously called the navel of the earth, a resting place for the Gods",* for more than a thousand years it has been a pilgrimage site for some of the world's major religions. The Hindus come to it from the south and the Bhuddists from Tibet and further afield. The monastic complex at Tholing was still functioning in 1966 when the Red Guards shut down operations and reduced most of it to ruins. But nevertheless, due to this contact with the Jesuits, the Guge Kingdom led a Bhuddist revival on the Tibetan plateau and became home to a hundred monasteries, most of them now in ruins.

Our *Kora,* or circuit, of Kailash will be 33 miles and take us over the Dolma La, which is at 18,569ft and normally takes about three days.

Many of the pilgrims prostrate themselves all the way round, in that way keeping contact with the earth, we will see one doing this.

The journey began, of course with a flight to Kathmandu, followed by an 11-hour overnight bus trip to Nepalganj, in the Terai or south of Nepal, from where we would take a small plane to Simikot in Humla before beginning our trek to Tibet. It was as recently as 1996 that the border was opened to allow foreigners to trek from Nepal into Tibet.

John writes: *"There was no time to contemplate the small size or steep slope of the grassy landing strip before we skimmed over a ridge in front with the stall klaxon shrieking and made a bumpy return to earth followed by instant breaking and clouds of dust"*. The plane did not linger due to the altitude, the airport is at 9,245ft and we and our bags hit the ground in more clouds of dust, and the plane took off again. Welcome to Simikot! (9,678ft)

18 September

As usual I get my bed tea half an hour before pax, at 5.30 a.m., so that I can be up and out. Helped Susan pack her stuff. Switchback trail. Lots of goats carrying salt bags and wool coming from Purang to Simikot. When they come past it is wise to climb a bank or a tree to avoid being trampled underfoot or pushed over the edge. In Humla the traditional salt and grain trade with Tibet continues much as it has for centuries. This trade has virtually ceased in the rest of Nepal because of the import of Indian salt and because China has eliminated many border trading posts in remote regions. The Humla Karnali is gushing through the gorge, below and we have lunch below a huge waterfall, which is good as it is 35°C. Susan and H have given their packs to the Sirdar and Sherpas, had hands held, and are way behind. This is worrying so early in a long trip. They should not be here but they are!

19 September

Decided I had to do something about Susan, as the further we got into the trip the longer it would take to get her out. Discussed this with her and she voiced her dread of doing those six days back. She is concerned that she might fall and damage her bad leg. She has also developed a huge raw blister, which we bound up this morning. Am aware she will not get insurance as this is an existing condition and I definitely feel I cannot send her back on her own with a Sherpa and a cook, and to find her own way back to Kathmandu. There is something ingenuous and naive about her and I am not sure how she would cope.

We decide to get her a horse for next three days and to keep her with us. I am concerned about the weather but we cannot walk at her pace for the rest of the trek. She says to me, "M.A., I am terrified of horses."

"Too bad, Susan, just get on!" John and I feel she deserves a chance to continue, and the group are supportive.

John writes: *"Last night was very special as we camped in the shadow of a big new gompa on the edge of the compound of a monastery built in 1984 and housing 70 monks. None of them appear to be older than perhaps 20, and many are young teenagers. They are a mixture of Nepalese and Tibetans. I had the extreme good fortune to arrive on my own just as they all streamed out for a break from a major service. They had been chanting, drumming and blowing trumpets with great gusto. They welcomed me and compared heights, many of them barely reaching chest height!"* (John is easily 6ft, M.A.)

"We all sat in the gloom of the temple, foggy with the scented smoke of burning cypress, watching them chant and trumpet. The youngest were given the job of drumming with curved sticks, and the two very youngest brought teapots to fill the jam jars secreted under the pews. The service was due to last three hours so we were invited upstairs (up a near vertical ladder) for tea and biscuits. We made a donation and put our names and size of our contributions in the official book. A charmingly bureaucratic gesture out here in the deserts of nearly Tibet."

Roger, John and I decided to share a beer and negotiated the price with the comic crone who owned the 'tea shop' and a group of her friends. She kept falling about as she dissolved into giggles and we all finished up in a sort of group hug while we swore to bring back a bottle of holy water on our return from Lake Manasarovar. These are the meetings that make Nepal so very special.

22 September

John and I have both caught fleas…I am covered in bites. Today we hoped to find the transport to take us on into Tibet. Of course the usual scenario. No transport, so we stay overnight below the Chinese frontier post, a small brick affair manned by two guards in uniform. We sheltered from the wind in their bedroom-cum-guardroom looking at family photographs and eating apples and melon (ours!). This was a very intimate affair, sharing family photographs in wild barren frontier surroundings, between Chinese guards far from China and home, and us...similarly placed. But the bond of parents and families dissolves all barriers.

Finally we drove for three quarters of an hour on very bumpy roads to Khojarnath Gompa on the way to Taklakot. It was a great sight to see all the inhabitants and their livestock winnowing the grain by walking on it in endless circles accompanied by shouts and songs. The beautiful village Gompa and the building surrounding it were truly medieval. The *mani* wall was topped by yak horns and carved yak skulls, as one finds on the roofs of houses in Dolpo. This is a Tibetan habit.

23 September

Taklakot is arid and colourful – ochres and creams with occasional stretches of pale green rivers.

John again. *"Roger and I have explored the town which is very spread out – a mixture of ghastly modern Chinese architecture intermixed with traditional mud and daub Tibetan houses. There were cave dwellings up behind the barracks but our climb up to them was delayed because two Chinese officers wanted to see that we were the people our passports showed us to be...we found a way through the army barracks and hospital into a market place full of colourful but non-Tibetan cheap clothing. Then across a prayer-flagged bridge to the caves and a Gompa with an extremely precarious balcony high up the cliff reached by stairs and a ladder. All the ceilings are very low so the top of my head suffered. R's head is conveniently slightly nearer the floor so it didn't!"*

We said goodbye to our pony men today, and Susan's horse, flogging up the Nara Lagna loaded up with Chinese wine of all things. We will meet them again when we return. The mind boggles at the thought of the wine coming from China to Lhasa and then on to this frontier post in far west Nepal.

We met four French folk tonight who had driven to Darchen by road from Lhasa (eight-12 hour days of driving!). They completed the

Kora without once seeing Kailash, it just poured with rain. I hope we are luckier.

24 September

We took a side trip here, before we went into Kailash. This was a first for the company, so very exciting.

After trekking from Nepal into Tibet we travelled west to Tsaparang and Toling, yet further and more remote. These two places are the ruined former capitals of the ancient Guge kingdom of Western Tibet. The Kingdom of Guge was founded in the 9th century. Buddhism was

reintroduced to western Tibet and the influence of the Guge Kingdom was felt from Kashmir to Assam. In 1624 the Jesuit, Father Antonio del Andrade, found his way to western Tibet from Goa. Essentially he converted so many to Catholicism that the local Bhuddists became alarmed and called in the neigh-

Tibetans at hot springs Tirtapuri

bouring kingdom of Ladakh to drive the new Christians from Tsaparang and the surrounding area. The Ladhakis lay siege to Tsaparang, overthrowing the king and imprisoning the Jesuits. This was the end of the Guge Kingdom. The Red Guards inflicted further destruction in 1947, when they destroyed statues and buildings, during the Cultural Revolution.

Just before we headed west we stopped at Tirtapuri. This is the third most important pilgrimage site for Bhuddists, a fantastic place with its steaming hot springs and salty secretions. John's diary again: *"The River Sutlej is crossed by strings of brightly coloured prayer-flags between cliffs which are themselves riddled with caves and topped by a Gompa, mani walls and chortens. Camping beside us are three truckloads of colourful Khampa people from the east of Tibet."*

The Khampas are a proud nomadic people and so did not suffer from the imposition of the Chinese on their way of life. This was an exciting place to be, with people making a *kora* round the water holes, and steam rising into the cold air. Just seeing these people climbing off their trucks with everything hung around them, was tremendously special. Decided we will stop here on our return as it is so exceptional.

The Khampas came originally from the east of Tibet, from an area called Kham abutting China. With the passage of time China has annexed Western Kham, which lies on the Chinese side of the Yangtse River. The people of Kham speak different languages to those of the people of Lhasa and have always been known to be warriors, renowned for their marksmanship and horsemanship. They helped the Dalai Lama to escape over the mountains to Nepal in 1959. Fiercely independent, they are also facially obviously different from the other occupants of Tibet. They have high cheekbones and a proud independent demeanour; they have tended to live as nomads, wandering the steppes of Tibet. For that reason the Chinese were never able to 'tame' them. Some of them settled in Ladakh during this time, but they are predominantly nomadic, instantly recognisable when you travel these parts. They are just strong, proud and good looking.

Our Sirdar is sick, but we are able to let him sleep it off, we hope, at Tirtapuri. We certainly need him on the *Kora*. Crowds of picturesque pilgrims arrive, and erect square low-slung tents with slits in the roof to let the smoke escape. This is a good place to take a little time out…we have to respect that our Sirdar has flu, though as the weather is good there is a feeling that we would like to have got going… but we can wash in the hot pools, not at all a bad idea, and take loads of photographs. As this was still the era of film, a general anxiety exists that we might run out.

25 September

Such a long day. Drove 11 hours, very bumpy road, narrow and twisting down canyon walls. Jack Rabbits and gazelles.

John writes: *"The sense of space is awe inspiring, emphasised as it is by the line of telegraph poles stretching to infinity. Sadly clouds have piled up above Kailash and the neighbouring peaks, but we did see the bottom of it, which is more than the poor French did. Roads on the plateau are seldom more than wheel tracks and we have seen only one other vehicle all day, two large jack rabbits, some distant herds of sheep and a nomadic family with their yaks.*

We are on our way to see Tsaparang, which must be one of the remotest towns on earth. Known as the capital of the 'Lost Kingdom of Tibet' it will be a 16 hour drive west from Taklakot, the nearest place which can qualify for the description of 'town', and goodness knows how many more than that to the west – Kashgar on the old Silk Road perhaps ...In front of us is a 180 degree unbroken panorama of the Himalayas from northern India to the Karakoram and on to the Pamirs. Nanda Devi is ahead and between us and it lies a truly amazing Grand Canyon of spires and gullies."

At Tholing we ate out, rice and noodles, at a Chinese 'hole in the wall' as everyone was exhausted. Someone's bag arrives swamped in kerosene, so I give her mine.

26 September

After a two-hour drive we come to Tsaparang. The Tsaparang citadel, or what remains of it, was built out of mud brick or hewn out of rock. It is indistinguishable from the other rocky pinnacles. The landscape here is a remarkable sight, characterised by deeply eroded sandstone and mud deposits. Great pinnacles, rocks and gullies have been cut out of the ancient soft layers.

We spend some hours exploring this unique place.

John writes: *"Breath taking, stupendous, hours of bone shaking travel were instantly forgotten. This is a 'converted mountain' created in the 10th or 11th century and abandoned for over 200 years, much of it is ruined, but the site and the buildings which have been restored, make this one of the world's wonders."*

We then drove four hours to camp beneath a stretch of stars. The weather is clearing so we keep our fingers crossed. No one here but us.

27/28 September

We drive to Darchen and my diary records, *"Darchen Guest House, four to a room, not bad. Ate in one room food prepared by Pasang. Loos foul, most people go behind the walls."*

After tea Roger, John and I climbed the ridge behind Darchen. We felt the height, 16,564ft but it should help us. After dinner H asked us all why we came on this trip and explained about the pilgrimage aspect for her and J. J was in tears…H is going to wear a white bandana on her arm to show us we must not talk to her. This only applied one way!

We see nomads here with their black tents folded on the backs of the sheep, and the tent poles bound in.

29 September

We pass a huge flagpole hung with prayer flags, and see Kailash peeping out. Susan is walking well, faster than H! I am feeling ill with the 'runs' so hide in my tent, but Roger and John visited another Gompa.

It is, or was, customary for a true pilgrim to make the entire *Kora* doing prostrations. This involves bending down to one's toes, and spreading one's body forward until flat on the ground, whereupon one brings one's feet up level with one's outstretched hands and stands up. The whole thing is repeated. Astonishing when one thinks that the distance for the *Kora* is close on 31 miles.

30 September

Susan's tent mate has a cold so have taken Susan in with me. She is doing fine and carrying her own pack. J approached me before

Prayer flags and Mt Kailash

Loading yaks

breakfast and asked me to send Susan back. I said I had absolutely no grounds to do so and the fact that Susan irritates J is no reason to do so. I stood my ground, oh the life of a leader! Its 17,515ft and John has lost his appetite and I am gulping for air! But I heard marmots!

1 October

Long day today. Nine hours. It had snowed during the night and was snowing in the morning. Could we go on? Sirdar said we would give it a go for an hour. One has a dilemma. If we do not go on, it could be worse tomorrow. We have limited food and an itinerary and eventually planes to catch. Really little option. H dropped back as soon as we began and was led by a Sherpa.

The Dolma La (18,569ft) was misty but a riot of colour from what is claimed to be the world's biggest collection of prayer flags. We walked for five hours down the valley, calling out *Tashi Delai* (hello) to

138

the other pilgrims, all of whom are wonderfully exotic in costume, jewellery and hairstyles and one lad is very proud of his straw hat. He is very handsome and knows it!

The day was rather spoilt for me after breakfast when I was called to the Canadians' tent and accused of ruining their *Kora* by not stopping at all the pilgrimage sites on the way round and not giving them enough time at the Dolma La. Had a lot of support from group who that felt the Canadians had been very selfish and possibly put the group at risk with their slow pace on the pass. Treks are all about compromise but it did spoil a lot of my day.

Roger noted in his own diary, *"Later I found myself walking behind H. As I came over a slight rise, I saw her in the dip below. She was alone, picking up stones, and hurtling them into the abyss. With each stone, she yelled 'Bloody Hell!' and 'Bitch' alternately. She was unaware of my presence, and so I stood there watching her for a full two minutes or more. Gradually she stomped off up the incline on the far side of the dip. As she did so, she glanced over her shoulder, and saw me..."*

No doubt this was directed at the leader!

Anyway, as we walk down we are met by our lorry and drive to Lake Manasarovar.

John writes, *"I think we left the shores of Manasarovar this morning with a lot of relief; last night was spent in deep sand accompanied by non-stop dog din. There were packs of them that wandered about howling all night."*

Before supper last night we visited the hilltop monastery perched above us on its outcrop with views of the lake and of a rather cloudy Kailash. While there we were joined by a truckload of happy pilgrims all the way from Amdo, north east of Lhasa, and the birthplace of the Dalai Lama. They were so colourful and we left them doing a *kora* round the rock.

And so we return to Taklakot along the path by which we came. We are waiting for lengthy negotiations to be completed so that the mules can cross the river and climb up to where the pile of our gear awaits them. We say goodbye to the truck and do up our bootlaces! Tomorrow is a 3,000ft ascent of the Nara Lagna which at this altitude is no easy stroll, and the track is unrelentingly steep.

Tibetans at lorry

John writes, *"To return to feelings about Tibet – it has been FAR more beautiful and exotic than I had expected. To have come all this way and not also to have travelled west to the Kingdom of Guge would have been a hugely missed opportunity. In some ways Tirtapuri and Tsaparang were even more of a highlight than Kailash because they combined stunning scenery and close contact with people and culture."*

I agree also that we enjoyed lots of birds, jack rabbits with their curious flap-like white tails, marmots, gazelles, a lone wolf and of course the wild dogs, who appear out of an apparently empty landscape and howl all night long!

5 October

The landscape is softening as we get further into Nepal, with pine trees and cotoneaster bushes. Pasang is cutting up potatoes and there is talk of chips so life looks good. John and I have got tired of cabbage and potatoes and are probably dreaming of a pepper steak in Kathmandu!

It was hard to fly out of Simikot and to find ourselves near Nepalganj once again, as here it was all flat, not what we are used to.

In Kathmandu we had a final dinner for all of us and our staff, after which to my shock Susan came to say she would be staying with one of our staff tonight 'at a hotel'(?) and was that alright with me!

All I said was, "Fine, have you got condoms?"…The work of a leader never seems to end! She is under the impression he wants to marry her. What can I say?

The transition sometimes longed for, is still hard to accommodate. A bed and hot water and a rich and varied menu can often make one long for…no, not potatoes and cabbage, but something simple and plain. This does not last long, and we are eating rich and varied fare once more. I have personally found when I arrive home I sometimes end up sleeping on the floor by my bed, until I get used to the idea of a mattress!

The Kingdom of Zanskar and the gorges
beyond the Charcha La, 1999

Walking up valley into Zanskar

A day in the life of a trek leader…just fun and sharing?

The brochure says, *"This is truly one of the finest long distance treks in the Himalaya. The prospect of undertaking this journey is at the same time both daunting, exciting and challenging. For the explorer in you, it is the stuff to make the adrenalin flow! It is something you will remember for the rest of your life."*…and that is for the clients…how about the leader…

Excerpts from my dairy say: *"We started up the Khurna Chu, we did eight crossings with rope, and one without, the water was above our knees and sometimes at crotch level. We had to do a terrifying Grade E9 high-level traverse, steps cut by Pasang with an ice axe in shale and sand, the rope useful for the first part, but after that you would swing like a pendulum should your foot slip. Bloody petrifying, above a cliff… everyone has been pushed to the very limit of their fear threshold. The clients were fantastic…I was a useless leader example, being last I was always left to get on with it and I was paralysed with fear, no rope for me."*

Added to that a horse got lame, and I thought we would have to shoot it. There was no food for the horses in the gorges, and then I lost my passport.

We journeyed from Delhi by train to Chandigarh, which was purpose built in the 1950s by le Corbusier. Chandigarh was intended to be the new capital of the Punjab, after Lahore was handed over to Pakistan, but never quite achieved the utopian, forward looking ideal of faith in a new India. We then boarded a bus and made our way to Manali at the head of the Kulu Valley, where I had been in 1969 on a personal expedition to climb Ali Ratni Tibba.

The road to Kulu was grim, with landslides, traffic jams and rides over rubble where the road had collapsed. Everyone was sheet white by Kulu. We were even staying at John Banon's Resort Hotel, which he developed from his cherry orchard we had visited 30 years earlier, after our ascent of Ali Ratni Tibba. Then I had gorged on his Sweetheart Cherries after our climb, savouring their sweet juiciness. Now we were a bit disappointed to find a huge TV in the bar with loud music and Star Trek movies.

Our bus crossed over the Rohtang La (14,500ft) the first major pass to be crossed by early Western explorers, and now a thriving little summit village of stalls selling socks, pendants and bracelets. We are on the notorious Leh to Manali highway, of which we had heard scary stories of narrow bends, drop offs and frequent trucks plunging over the side. We might have been happier walking!

After finally getting to the start of the trek, my diary will pick up the story, in its some-times graphic detail, of beautiful wild empty country, flowers, and isolation. And frights.

"Great views over to Spiti and Lahul. Lots of workers from Bihar pouring tar on roads, crushing rocks etc. Edelweiss at the roadside, a wagtail and a

Prayer flags and mountains of Zanskar

weasel, then a plumbeous redstart. The backdrop is the rugged gran-deur of rocky mountains and hanging glaciers. Juniper bushes now and willows by the Bhaga River. A grey wagtail at the edge. Potatoes every-where and buckwheat. Farmers making huge stacks of fodder on roofs of houses, as they do in Tibet. The colours are striking. Oranges, browns and beiges in the rock and sand punctuated by edelweiss and the strik-ing blue of a solitary gentian. 'Full many a flower is born to blush unseen and waste its sweetness on the desert air'. Our first camp night. Four yellow North Face tents, Sherpa crew and cook! Everyone finds it very funny that I speak some Nepali and I wish I had brought my phrasebook. The crew are young and it's wonderful to hear them laugh-ing and singing. John Lama is a good Sirdar I think, and as we don't have a cook crew here in Zanskar, we have two Sherpas who produce tasty food. (The career path for a Sherpa, is baggage carrier, cook, then Sherpa helping clients and perhaps finally Sirdar.)

I am looking forward to tomorrow when we have our first river crossing, on a horse! It was cold in the mess tent tonight and I wished I had brought warm trousers.

We are at 14,000ft, clients in various states of disarray. Maggie, a very experienced walker, worldwide and also in Scotland, has the shakes, has a headache and is out of breath walking from the tent. Mel is not peeing at all, despite giving her Diamox, a mild diuretic. A build-up of liquid at altitude is a suspicious sign and after about 10,000 feet fluid retention can become apparent in swollen hands, ankles and under the eyes. It can develop into serious high altitude problems and death if not dealt with and alleviated. The best remedy is descent, but this is not always possible. Diamox can help until one is acclimatized. (I am con-sulting Peter Steele's definitive book on Altitude Sickness). I am worried. Her resting pulse is 104, mine is 60. She also has giardia. Decisions, decisions. Either we get her over the pass, on a horse if necessary, and down to lower ground in the main Zanskar Valley, or we have to send her back to Manali and Delhi. A daunting prospect. The pass we are aiming for is the Phirtse La and is 17,876ft. This is quite a rise in altitude from Delhi, in nine days. On the other side, in the Valley we are 6,000ft lower. There Mel would probably recover and get used to a, relatively speaking, lower height. It's a tough start for a tough trek. But of course at this stage I do not know just HOW tough. Pasang takes her rucksack.

Huge day. We stopped every 30 minutes to collect everyone and to have a drink. Mel looked a terrible colour and I tried to get a horse but the ponymen said, "No, horse was tired". We didn't see the horses again till near the top. Judy said, 'This is like a marathon, it takes guts and determination to get to the end. Mel is sick again. We stopped for a break once we were over, and then learnt it was another four hours to camp. Mel exhausted. I sent for a horse again, and an hour from camp one arrived, but Mel was scared and refused to get on. So we trudged on. When we got to camp, I put her in her tent, in a bag and gave her some boiled water. Later on she had two soft-boiled eggs mushed up with butter and some Dioralyte, rehydration powder. Amazing she made it, in a way she had no choice.

The rest of us had a large supper of dal, rice, vegetable curry, momos and sauce. Judy felt sick and did not eat. But we got over the pass. Someone produced some Longmorn Glenlivet, and we crawled off to our tents and collapsed. Next day we had a big river crossing. John Lama brought two horses down, and the men leading the horses staggered thigh deep in the water, hanging on to the bridles. I was put up on the front of the wooden saddle and the Zanskar boy was behind me. I suggested he grabbed my waist – he did – then grabbed my groin. As we left the bank the horse tried to buck. Pasang was thoroughly enjoying this and leapt onto a horse and urged it into a canter towards the tents. It threw him off, rucksack and all. Much merriment. Major washings at camp of clothes and hair and as the water was quite warm, we have no headaches washing our hair".

This is a wide valley after the passes, which seem to guard entrance to this wild place. There are more flowers, thyme and potentilla, but most flowers are over. We saw marmots, then a hoopoe scrounging under rocks and plants, probably for bugs, a wheatear type bird and a wagtail. On the higher slopes I saw a lot of yaks grazing, and a tiny herd of *kyang* (wild asses). It is a truly awesome, wild landscape of wide plateaux, and craggy snow peaks, but also grassy meadows, delicate flowers, blue skies and meandering streams.

House with solar panel and
yak dung fuel

We become a curiosity. Four ladies of varying ages come from the yak herders' tents which are made of woven yak hair, one lady has a baby on her back. Some dressed in traditional *chubas*, others in Western clothes, a wee boy wears an old Snoopy sweatshirt. Mel had the great idea of showing them postcards, and photos so we ushered them into a tent, let them look through binoculars, and Judy let them watch a video replay on her camera. An old lady of 60 with eye problems turned up, so I put in some eye drops, which nipped a bit, but soothed her. I was very moved at her kneeling, trusting, at my feet in the mess tent. Just like the old turbaned men in Morocco, who also had eye problems. In the midst of this wildness and bareness, there is a shared feeling of trust and giving. After this the little group headed off to our cook tent, and we heard drumming and singing, then they left and went home in the hail and rain, which we have become accustomed to each afternoon.

These nomadic people live a traditional life, herding *pashm* goats and sheep, milking the yaks and the goats, which also supply them with meat and wool. The under wool of these Tibetan sheep is used in the making of Pashmina shawls, and in fact *pashm* is the Old Persian word for cashmere goats. The wool of these goats was brought down from Tibet into India through Ladakh and Zanskar in the 19th century. There was a thriving trade in Paisley shawls in India.

Mel's gear must draw amusement from the crew. When it rained she proudly donned a plastic mac with 'Villiger Swiss Cigars' printed on the back. Her sleeping bag is Hollofil, when everyone else has goose down RAB bags, but she says she is warm enough with her space blanket on top. I am glad of my RAB four season bag.

The main valley is a wide flood plain, it is opening up to left and right with our first sight of civilisation, tilled fields and houses. The barley sheaves are laid out so that the actual head of one sheaf is under the roots of the other to keep it dry, I suppose. Potatoes are in walled enclosures, with dung laid out to dry on the roofs. Glass in tiny windows. An old crone invited me in to the barley field to help her cut the grain. There were water channels, donkeys and a chained dog barking frantically, so I kept out of sight. We saw horses with huge bags, apparently this is flour. A lot of men go on trek, as in Nepal, to make money to buy the flour to keep them going for a year, leaving the women and old men to tend the harvest. Lots of *mani* walls here, and lots of peas and barley growing. The children use peapods to barter for sweeties. Where the yaks are grazing the women follow them with huge baskets, picking up the dung and making it into wide flat cakes, which they store in the baskets to be used as fuel. We even saw a loom in one village. Resting at our

Women tossing straw

lunch spot in a barley field trying to avoid the cold wind, we were joined by four wee kids and so gave them the remains of our lunch, puris and an apple. This is a wonderful place to be.

We met a miserable, boring Englishman and his Hong Kong girl-friend. For him everything was wrong, the ponymen, the horses, the trail. He depressed my joyous spirits a bit. I was happy with the freedom, space, fresh air, wonderful mountains and simple people, living simple but hard lives, who sing and laugh. I often used to find my whole soul would expand in these open spaces.

On our way we visited the *gompa* at Phuktal. There were two paths. The one we trod followed an airy path along the side of the gorge above the Zanskar River where the towering rocks glowed orange in the sunlight. Often the path was hewn out of the rock face. I had a look at the alternative route. Variously described as 'scary', 'impossible for horses' with loose scree to be run across to connect with the path. Not a chance for us, and as a rule of thumb I decided if the horses can't manage a path, neither should we.

Phuktal Gompa is incredible. It is perched high up on a cliff face and seems to tumble down the mountainside, with the main part of the temple inside a cave. We were offered toasted barley by a monk at the gate and as we entered we met many young boys and a wee lad of two who had just arrived, his father had died and his mother

Wee boy at Phuktal

was blind. They did all seem quite scruffy, and I found it all a bit creepy. But on reflection, what a life, on the side of a cliff, in the cold, water to be fetched from the river below, no heat. Food? We met a French girl who had come to stay for the eighth time and tries to teach them. She says the teacher is often away. An old man came wanting something for his bad back and arthritic knees, so we gave him two Nurofen.

In the top temple I found a lot of murals, painted by Kashmiri artists, which, Judy says, are like those in Tsaparang, in Tibet, which I visited in 1998. The views down the valley from this *gompa* emphasise the width of the valley, surrounded by mountains, all bare, and all brown, and grey, rock and scree. The light is astonishing: dark shadows alternate with flashes of gold light on the mountains, flashes of blue rivers, and patches of green fields.

On our way to camp we passed a wolf trap. These are low stone rings with no exit, into which a piece of meat is thrown, and this encourages the wolves who then cannot get out, as the stone walls lean inwards.

A long trudge along the valley brings us to Padum, capital of Zanskar, and we are now half way. There are waders in the lake, but I am too tired to bother. Padum is fifty per cent Muslim so is dominated by a big silver shiny Mosque. A surprise. The other surprise is a 'campground' of grass, willows and a standpipe for extensive laundry washing. There are three grain mills beside a rushing stream at the side of the campsite.

My list of jobs in Padum says:

1. *One horseman leaves us here and returns to Manali. 500 Rs tip.*
2. *Arrange for tomorrow, visit to King, visit to Karsha Gompa by local jeep (clients to pay)*
3. *Inquire about renting horse/saddle and ponyman for Judy (and Mel) for the Charcha La, the next pass 17,000ft. Judy says the route march yesterday, "was not a holiday" and she used a horse in Dolpo.*
4. *Warn pax about keeping valuables away from tent sides at night, in sleeping bag or locked kitbag.*
5. *Toilets are foul, put up toilet tent*
6. *A Sherpa has come through from Nimaling (other side of Gorges, in Ladakh) and says all is ok, water levels are low. These can rise suddenly after rain, so one can be trapped.*
7. *Go for a beer!*

Next day we took the jeep to Karsha Gompa. Found it pretty filthy, lots of old monks in dirty red *chubas* and a wee lad of about ten. It was hard to believe what I read in the *Lonely Planet* guidebook that there are *"150 monks, subject to the control of the younger brother of the Dalai Lama"*. Three old monks did a ceremony in the courtyard, blessing balls of *tsampa*, while eight dogs lay snoozing.

Visited Phunchok Namgyal, King of Padum. Very friendly, he teaches at the High School, with about 80 children. We sat in his kitchen with a single light bulb dangling down, and asked him questions about Zanskar and the solar panels we have seen frequently. We gave him a *kata*, a ceremonial white scarf of friendship, when we left. I had to dash for cover…my turn for the runs, running. Swallowed some Ciproxin.

Leaving Padum for Zangla we passed another Gompa, Thonde. I did not visit due to my gut rot, but Judy spent two hours in there and pronounced it to be 'stupendous', had been given butter tea and *tsampa*. It was freshly painted, and flowers were growing in the courtyard. There is a nunnery here, founded by nuns who escaped from Tibet at the same time as the Dalai Lama, and there is an old Fort surrounded by white *chortens*. Nice spot. We camped in grounds of the 'palace', the king was in Leh. Water here comes from a pipe that dries up during the afternoon! It is worth reflecting that in winter the frozen Zanskar River becomes the highway for those wanting to visit Leh, as this is the only route out in winter. It takes a week, and one sleeps in caves along the way. A friend of mine has done it, and was blackened by soot for weeks afterwards, as they lit fires in the caves at night.

Man with horse, prayer flag and empty hills

'Goodbye Culture – Hello wilderness'

This is the start of the Gorges. But first we must cross the Charcha La. Another day another pass. Or so I thought, but on this our starting day we found we had to cross the river, the Zumling Chu, about thirty times. Sandals are high priority, and good ones. For three hours we waded the river or scrambled along the edge of the canyon, which has no shore, until we were able to put our boots on and having arrived at a willow grove with cliffs towering 1,000ft above us, we fancied some lunch. But the horses, which we need for this part of the trip, have not turned up. They are carrying our food and tents. They were expected at six but by 8 p.m. there was no sign of them, so John Lama and Pasang retraced our route to look for them. Had the ponymen pulled out, as it is such a hazardous trip? They probably didn't fancy it one bit. Preparing for such an emergency, it was decided John Lama and all the Sherpas would go back and carry provisions up to where we were, and I found a stone shelter and laid in firewood! Not needed.

The ponymen turned up later and we put tents up below soaring cliffs. Apparently the horses had gone off in search of grass. It's very difficult ground for horses, narrow, loose, rocky paths and no food. One horse hit a tree and crushed a box containing peppers, carrots and aubergines. The three hens had a rough ride in their basket on top of a horse, but were released, fed and watered! Clients very supportive over the horse problem, but now Maggie is trying to ward off a chest infection, Mel is tetchy and the Ciproxin seems to have beaten my bug! All looks good.

It seems Mel came on this trip as it was the cheapest she could find...to Zanskar.

She complains she is lonely on this trip, as after tea we all go to our tents till supper, the Sherpas sing, but as she tends to tell us all about all her trips, most people seek relief in their tent, I certainly do, by 8.30 p.m.! I arranged for her to join the crew next day when they are singing, so perhaps she will get some 'fun'! (Leader not getting a lot of 'fun' either, imagining a rescue in here...no chance, a helicopter could not get here, it would be a long carry on a horse.)

One day down and four to go! The Charcha La day. Mel had her bag carried all day by a Sherpa, Techi, the rest of us staggered up the scree for four hours, but the last hour the path zigzags back and forth amongst rocks and hard earth. John Lama made steps with his ice axe and both Judy and Mel were led by the hand. Judy put up prayer flags on the top. The horses turned up. How do they manage it? Chocolate and photographs, then it's down. Much easier than we had been led to believe, just three long zigzags on the scree.

We stopped for lunch after half an hour and then continued down. The gorge is awesome, towering red rock faces 1,000 feet up on both sides, lots of snow bridges and avalanche debris to navigate. It is very narrow for about 160 yards and you are forced up, about 60ft above the gorge for about an hour, quite scary, more steps cut with ice axe. Definitely not for anyone not used to rough walking.

Finally arrived at Tom Tokh Sumdo, an oasis in the midst of all this real rock. Water is ice cold, willows shiver in the breeze but provide a glimpse of green in this red and grey wilderness, everyone exhausted and one of the horses is quite lame. (Will we have to shoot it if it cannot walk?) Two hens are still with us, did we already eat one? I gave them some water and Pema covered them with a sack for shelter.

A long day watching feet and path. All a bit tired of stunning gorge scenery and river crossings. Some had to be waded and some leapt over on slippery submerged rocks. Rhubarb grows here, and wild chives, and I recognise silver birch trees.

Into camp, lame horse now has a nosebleed, but is limping unladen except for its bag of grass, horseman has giardia and is lying down. No grass for horses here, not that there is ever much. Viv Bahadur is unwell, headache, dizzy, diarrhoea. It's taking its toll. Gave horseman some Tiniba, Judy gave him an iron pill, next three days are really hard. Not a lot we can do, just go on and get out. Mel thinks she is the living authority on giardia, it's grating on my nerves.

September 11, Saturday: This was not only a very long day, it was also a terrifying day that put the word 'adventure' among the Boys Own league, a rope is absolutely essential today.

The usual descent along the gorge, 26 river crossings, in three hours. After lunch we came to the junction of the Zumling Chu and the Khurna Chu. This is an amazing open place, like a cathedral almost, with the canyon opening up three ways and sheer walls, an alluvial gravel plain and a sign on a rock saying Zanskar with arrows pointing both ways…?

We met a Dutch couple with three ponies starting up the Zumling Chu. She said it had been very scary and dangerous. We started up the Khurna Chu, and did eight crossings with a rope and one without, water at crotch level, and flowing fast. Then we had to do a terrifying high-level traverse, with steps cut into the scree and sand with an ice axe; we used the rope to secure the first part, after that, if you fell you swung. Of course being the last, I had no rope. Bloody petrifying above a cliff...I think we all wondered if we would get out of here alive.

We are all looking forward to Nimaling, the end. Folk have been pushed to the very limit of their fear threshold.

Clients were fantastic. Judy burst into tears of relief, but all joked and laughed, at surviving...as chicken hits our supper table.

The end is closer, everyone is worn out, moving very slowly. At camp cook made us omelettes and rice, but I was not well, shivering, headache and pulse rate 88, and managed little. I think it has all been too much.

We had had to send the horses round a different way for the last pass and when they arrived they neighed with delight to see their friends again. Signs of less remote area here, an empty cigarette packet, a sweetie paper, and two South Africans with three bony Ladakhi horses. John Lama says the Ladakhi horses are always thin, no grass grows here, and so they are not capable of what our strong Manali horses did. Even the lame horse is walking now. Thankful reprieve.

Second last day...but when I checked for my passport, it was not in my tent, it was not anywhere. Ransacked tent, sleeping bag, and rucksack. This was not a good moment. I will never leave Ladakh, never mind India! Anyway, on my tearful admission to crew Passang left for Leh, via Hemis, to organise pick up jeeps for us, and to give my passport details (N.B. Always carry a photocopy of your passport!) to Rimo, our agent in Leh, who will sort it all. These guys are amazing, nothing throws them.

On a brighter note we spent some time watching a herd of blue sheep with huge horns, on the far bank of the river and saw snow leopard footprints on the path. We saw Tibetan snowcock, they do not like to fly, being big birds, the size of a turkey. Also wagtails, a wheatear and a raven. More herds of yak, goats and sheep and a teahouse tent, where Mel offered to buy a sheep for our supper!

Leh is closer now.

Looking down the Marka Valley, the hills now are purple, less red, and we had superb views of the hanging glaciers of Kang Yatse, a trekking peak, 21,000ft, it was exciting to see a snowy hill again.

The mood changes. Gentians, and edelweiss grow everywhere. Wildlife abounds. Mel found some snow leopard's pelt, we saw *Lammergeiers*, griffon vultures, a weasel and lots of curious marmots whistling their warning. The horses have gone miles during the night and the horseman gets up at 5.30 a.m. to look for them. After the horrors of the gorge, they must love the limitless space where there might be grass.

We divided our worn and dirty clothes into bags to distribute amongst the crew, sorted out tips and then had a last camp supper, made special by Maggie producing some fruit and nut chocolate, and a bottle of Bruachladdich. We had spring rolls, and cake. I made my speech in stilted Nepali and the boys danced the traditional Nepali dances of Risum Piriri and Pankopat to the music of the singing. Good fun.

Our last walking day, towards Leh, we leave Lato behind and are on a tarred road. The crew are preening themselves, washing their hair and finding crushed clean trousers to sport in Leh. There are a few houses now, barley is harvested. Judy and I spent a happy time waiting for the horses, watching a mother and daughter winnowing, singing in time. Two little children were sitting on a coat amongst the sheaves, and further over horses are walking round and round a pole, treading on the cut grain, and threshing it to the sound of more singing, and with a wee foal following behind. What a timeless scene, I felt so at peace here, and despite the last few days, do not want to leave this place. I love the simplicity and freedom of these villages, and the people are kind and cheerful and laugh and sing. When one thinks of home...

On jeeps to Leh and checked into the hotel. Day passed shopping, and me reporting my lost passport to the police...where did you lose it? *Muezzin* are calling and reminding me of the large Muslim population here. With two clients went to see a video of Helena Norberg-Hodge's book *'Ancient Futures, Learning from Ladakh'*. This is a book trying to show us how to move into globalisation without losing the simplicity of living. Here is a short extract.

'Leh was capital of Ladakh in the 17th century, and was once an integral part of Western Tibet, and a major trading post along the Southern Silk Route, linking with Skardu and Kargil. Caravans of traders from far flung destinations such as Yarkand, Tibet, Kashgar and North India passed through Leh on ancient trade missions, trading salt,

wool, Pashm, tea. Pilgrims flocked to the monasteries of Leh and explorers of old stopped here to restock and weather out the harsh Himalayan winter.'

Next day Chewang Motrup of Rimo took us to the airport and we found, as expected, we could not fly with our baggage, as the priority is to get the people out, and at this altitude the plane cannot take off with too much weight. Leh stands at 11,562ft. I had thoughts of our baggage finally reaching us some time later in Heathrow, but there was no way round it. One woman in another party got her bag, as she had a medical problem but I could not invent five medical problems.

The flight is spectacular, over the Indus River, which rises on the Tibetan plateau and reaches the sea at Karachi. If you know what you are looking for you can see K2, Nanga Parbat and Gasherbrum.

The rest is unimportant, but I did spend the whole day in Delhi being whistled between the British Consulate, and the Government Office to leaf through a large ledger where everyone's name is written, who has landed at the airport until we found mine. I had entered India. I had a new passport, and flew home.

This passport caused me to be retained in Los Angeles in 2004… but that's another story, as they say, I had no machine readable data.

Chapter Six
Episodes

Three snow gullies before lunch, 1976

"Why don't we just go down the Goat Track and do another one? That was magic!" Carol looked at me…high on freedom and excitement, the sun shone, the sky was blue, there was no wind and the snow was in perfect condition, hard névé. My nostrils tingled as I smelled the keen, cold air.

Carol McNeill and I had climbed several snow gullies in our time, and I had soloed several 'easy' ones in the Cairngorms loving the freedom of climbing solo, without that tugging rope…moving at my own pace and carefully looking ahead and judging the ground, watching for anything coming down the gully towards me. One hears every small sound, a tumbling ice crystal breaks the silence as it bounces and rolls past. Being alone one is more aware.

So on with the crampons, out with the axe, stepping up the slope on the front points, so simple! With our combined amount of mountaineering experience we were not really stepping so far out of line, except that I was a now a mother!

So on this occasion, as the children were at school, and I had a morning free, I was enthusiastic to join Carol and go into Coire an t-Sheachda to climb a gully in an area called The Trident. There are three routes in there – the Runnel, Crotched Gully and Central, which oddly enough, lies to the left of the other two. Each one is about 300ft in length. I had climbed them all previously but roped and one at a time!

We each had a rucksack with the gear required; a rope, some pegs and carabiners so that we could put in some protection as we passed by the rock walls. But when we reached the bottom of the Runnel, we thought we would just try it without the gear…and we did! We shot to the top and out onto the sunny plateau. So easy!

We couldn't resist it; we went down and did another, this time Crotched Gully. And of course we HAD to finish the day by doing the last one, Central…There was a difficult moment, as this gully does tend to have an ice section, not much, but my memory tells me it was about six feet in height. Vertical. I had a moment of indecision. "Carol, can I tie on once you are up?"

"You have the rope, MA."

Realisation. Think positive and do it!

What a day! We still remember that day, and the fact that, as I had promised to take the kids out to tea, I had to hurry down the Fiacaill of Coire Cas to get back to the car and Glenmore Lodge where I lived. My husband Fred was pacing the car park, not a happy man. But we had had our unforgettable day!

Thanks Carol! I don't think either of us ever repeated that sort of day again!

Skiing on the Cairngorms from a helicopter, 1975

The bird flies high and we are inside. Skis wedged door to door, we sit back on upturned ski edges, crouching down, waiting to find the ideal slope. Words spoken and comments made are lost as the rotor blades spin round and round. The pilot speaks into his mouthpiece but no one knows the question he asks except one who also has earphones and a mouthpiece, and he nods and mouths words that we miss. I face the back but crane round to see where we go not what we leave behind. No deer. All is white and empty. Only the lower passes, streambeds and coires trace black lines on the white canvas. We whirl forward up the tunnel of the Lairig Ghru, and steep sides close in as we move forward, and into Glen Geusachan and up on to the Monadh Mor.

The helicopter ceases its forward momentum and descends amidst a cloud of flying snow, to rest gently on the frozen ground. We push the doors open. Sticks and skis are tossed out, and the rucksack with first aid hurls through the air to roll on the snow and stop against a rock. We throw ourselves out next, sliding forward to the open door as we cannot stand on the helicopter's floor, which is too slippery for the soles of our plastic ski boots. Out, heads down, we scurry below the deadly head-chopping blades, flying snow spray and wind, until we are clear.

The helicopter rises and goes. The pilot nods and slides the plane down through the air, downhill to where he will find us seven minutes from now! Skis on, bindings click, hands through the straps, push the poles and off we go. Each of us anywhere on this wild open slope, searching for freedom through gravity, searching for thick snow, hard icy snow, good edge holding snow. Good turns then a drift of waxy powder, swinging down, holding one's own line, no one has ever skied this bit before, whoopee, everyone skiing his way, his style, his ability. We stop…we are in the midst of silence and emptiness, awesome. Suddenly we hear the chopper below us, let's go.

Superb – Sgoran Dubh Mor, Glen Feshie, Cairn Toul, Coire Gorm. It's over, down to the last trickle of fuel we head back home. This has been a dream in the clouds on the tops, a dream of freedom and self, and in an encapsulated world where one can be anything and shout for joy and the exhilaration of free ski borne flight.

On the flight deck with Peter Harper 1999

In 1996, my elder son, Peter, had been privileged to spend six months in the Antarctic with the British Antarctic Survey. While there he co-piloted a small plane and when he returned announced he would like to be a pilot. He 'chased' sponsorship for two years and finally was awarded it with Air 2000, with whom he still flies, though they are now called Thomson Airways. He has moved from flying a Cessna to a Boeing 757, then to the Dreamliner, and now he is a Captain flying 737s. This is an account of a trip I flew with him in 1999.

Day dawns. 4.30 a.m. and pre alarm. I creep downstairs, kettle on, cats round my feet for early morning breakfast. Mug of tea. Peter comes in, "Mum, I've got a surprise for you, you're going to Crete today not Malaga!" Fine with me. Peter has arranged for me to go on his flight, on the flight deck, with him and the captain. Of course since 9/11 this is now off limits

Off through dark pre-dawn on country roads. A frog hops across a deserted lane, a shocked owl sits staring on the white line before winging it over the hedge and then a fox scurries under a fence near the airport. The belly of a plane skims the rooftops of houses that lurk below the flight path to Manchester Airport.

We park the car, meet John Grogan, Peter's captain for today, and I am issued a ticket for the Flight Deck.

The clients for this flight have overnighted locally, as someone had inadvertently pushed the steps too close to the plane and damaged the door. Now we are repaired and ready to go. More delays, the captain's headset is not working; that is fixed but we have not enough water on board for the toilets. This side of the 'Flight Curtain' it all seems to flow quite seamlessly, but if you are sitting in the cabin with 230 other passengers it seems yet another boring hold up!

Time to go. We are manoeuvred backwards and taxi forward, bump, bump, onto the runway, line ourselves up with the lights and go. Today Peter has chosen to be the pilot flying out, and John will be the pilot bringing the plane back, with each of them playing a support role and listening to air traffic control on the flight. Peter wants the experience of difficult landings, and Heraklion on Crete is tricky. I am sitting in the jump seat right behind the Captain, John, and he and Peter sit side by side, checking with one another each thing that they do, speed, height as we rise, watching the altimeter, set for 20,000 ft. We rise a lot faster than climbing hills…5,400ft, 5,470ft.

Through the clouds, Peter and John talking through their headsets and checking, thumbs up from John. Peter pressing buttons, switching knobs, John checking radio, weather, etc. Peter has plotted the route and fed it into the computer and you can follow our progress on a small screen on the dashboard. We are a small triangle, moving imperceptibly up a line, with dots representing airports to the right and left.

Nicky, Cabin Crew number one, opens the door to the Flight Deck, "Would you like a cup of tea? And there's a spare breakfast M.A., do you want it?" Since it is now 8.30 a.m. and a long time since breakfast with the cats, I say, "Yes, please".

John and Peter discuss flights and 'CBs' – cumulonimbus, thunderstorms, that can suddenly appear on a flight, something to watch out for. Peter showed me how the Alps (high ground) appears on radar, which shows up thunderstorms, the radar reflects off the water in them.

We are travelling at ground speed of 550mph and are 37,000ft up using four tons of fuel per hour. All is set on the computer, so after Paris we turn left, and the plane tilts itself and goes. Seems weird. We are over a blanket of stratus and see nothing, but above us the sun shines.

Our flight out is over Eastbourne, Paris and Geneva where it is raining, as it is in Milan. It's sunny up here but turbulent and I find myself wondering how those at home are faring. Peter's wife has a new baby. Peter and John appear not to do anything, the plane just flies. Everything is automated but backed up, manual overrides.

Meanwhile the passengers are watching a video (it's more fun on the Flight Deck). A sea of faces greets me when I go to the toilet. It's cosy and light in the cockpit with Nicky popping in and out, and it will never be the same again in a passenger seat.

The clouds part as we cruise above the east coast of Italy and we make out the 'heel', and Peter speaks over the Tannoy, "This is the First Officer speaking, over to the right you can see Mount Etna, and on our left is Brindisi. We have just passed over Corfu.' I see a stream of cloud floating out from Etna and the islands below are floating in a blue and choppy sea. I am alarmed to see a plane below us, going north. 1,000mph combined speed, with exhaust streaking out behind.

Half an hour out of Crete we start our descent. Peter set the altitude to be dropped to, and the plane obeys. "Boeing did a good job," says John, "But they don't do the difficult bits," Peter quips. Solid cloud over Crete with just the high mountains pushing through. How does Peter keep his cool? It looks a craggy coastline as I see through a gap in the clouds. Peter wants the practice of landing at these awkward places. "Do you want an extended visual?" asks John. Peter says yes, and so we approach along the coast. "Good for windsurfing today" says John. It's very stormy.

4,500ft wheels down, oops, we approach, reduce speed, down to 2,500ft. We are five miles out still (we cover two miles a minute). I can see cars and people. Quite a headwind. We line up. Over the cliffs that mask the headland. It's quiet in here, dare I even breathe? Bounce, bounce and we are down. John says: "Well done Peter, great approach. You don't get two chances!" What a buzz it must give Peter to get it right, and there was a strong crosswind. I am very proud.

Peter and I went out to check plane, tyres, and brakes. Then we put in 18 tons of fuel. I am overwhelmed by the size of the fuselage and am told to be aware of where I am. As indeed I am.

There is a 55-minute turnaround. Greek ladies have hoovered the plane and removed the rubbish. The girls have gone through the inflight magazines and replaced them. They ask me if I am proud of Peter. I am. It's windy and grey here today and I have no desire to stay, more food is loaded, new passengers stream on and it's time to go. Peter gives me a pair of headsets so I can tune in to Air Traffic Control as we move from airspace to airspace. It is all very fast and our call name is 'Jet Set 467 Delta' so I don't take a lot in, but the man from Maastricht is very friendly, "Bye bye".

We go back over Athens, Corfu, then up the coast, but the visibility is bad, so I read a magazine. How laid back I have become. Cheese and biscuits appear and I tussle with a Granny Smith apple and a plastic knife. ATC and making lists of airports we pass over, in case we need to make an emergency landing. Over England there are threatening clouds and constant messages from pilots asking to change direction a few degrees to, "avoid the weather".

John leaves Peter and me alone on the Flight Deck for a few minutes. This is an odd feeling for me, at 31,000ft, alone with my son. Flying home.

We line up with the lights of Manchester Airport and come in over the roofs of the houses we passed this morning and drive home to find Stephanie has prepared our roast chicken.

Fantastic day.

Peter the Pilot

Out on the edge, a Chamonix gully with Peter, 2000

I followed Peter off the open smoothly groomed ski run, into new powder, and onto a steep slope with bumps and rocks either side, narrow and leading down to a narrow rocky gully. The sunny, populated ski run was off to the right, gentle and appealing. Why am I here? I look down, terrified. My mind takes it in…if I slip here I will plunge on down this slope and over into the gully. Certain death. I turn round carefully and start, very determinedly, to 'herringbone' (climb) back up to where we began our descent, the top of the chairlift. Snow cascades past me.

Peter says, "Come on, Mum, I will go below you". So I obey. My mind tells me again that this is mad…if I slip I take him with me. Then we both go down the slope, inch by inch, stepping horizontally sideways, making sure the ski edge bites.

How did I get here? It began as a pleasant ski trip with my son, Peter, and his wife, expecting their first child, and now I am side stepping down a steep slope, with rocks either side, and a gully below. I move slowly, digging in the steel edges of my skis.

Slowly and thinking only of each side step, we make it to the bottom. I am facing the wrong way. The gully yawns below. I have to turn round. I do – a star turn…turning crabwise till I am round.

I follow Peter onto the carefully groomed slope and whizz in perfect parallel turns to the bottom. When I express my horror at where we were he says: "But Mum I thought you had done lots of things like this!!" I had taught skiing in Valmorel in France, and often skied off piste in powder on my own, but somehow this was a step further. My spirit flew high in relief into the sunshine and the trees! My whole inside expanded!

We were down. We joined Stephanie, quite unaware and sitting in the sun below a spreading larch tree.

CHAPTER SEVEN
Time with Chris Brasher and Sailing the *'Eda Fransen'*

OBOE: Chris formed a small company of friends whom he considered to be like-minded people and proposed to create outings planned as Eric Shipton was famously apt to do, "On the Back Of an Envelope," thus emphasising the informality of setting up an adventure!

I was lucky enough to be elected to be one of his august band and we had many small outings in the OBOE outline. I think it may have been my friendship with Carol MacNeill who was British Orienteering Champion many times, and her friendship with Chris, whose article for *The Observer* in 1957 had championed Orienteering, that contributed to my being invited. But then I also knew Eric Langmuir very well (of Mountain Leadership fame, his book being the recognised Bible of aspiring mountain leaders). Eric had been at Cambridge with Chris.

The following is a typical example of an OBOE outing.

I am preparing supper in the kitchen, guests at the table, the phone rings, "M.A., Chris here, can you come to Glen Affric tomorrow? I am coming up on the train tonight with Ken Ledward and we are going to Glen Affric. I want to test some outdoor clothes I am designing and want you to model them for me on the hill!" This was typical Chris…he had an idea…jump to it! Ken was well known as Ken Ledward Equipment Testing Services (KLETS) but was also a good friend of Chris.

So I went and met Chris and Ken at the Cluanie Inn. After a delicious meal and entertaining chatter from Chris as usual regaling us with many funny happenings, we went to bed.

Next morning Carol MacNeill joined me and we strode up from the Cluanie Inn into the heather and wind on An Caorann Beag, below the Five Sisters of Kintail. Chris behind the lens of his camera, and wind blowing our hair everywhere, I laughed at the pleasure of my day out, however silly it seemed sprawling in the heather, whilst wearing one of Chris's fleeces made out of plastic bottles.

A pleasant evening was spent in the Inn, good food, wine and conversation. An evening with Chris was always full of laughter, stories, memories and plans.

Of the very many memories of I have of him, these are a random selection which I hope give an indication of the breadth of his achievements.

He invited me to sail on a rubber boat to St Kilda with him and Ken…but I was unable to go. A missed opportunity.

I spent time with Chris in the Lake District walking north to south in a group made up of friends he had met here and there, coming for a day here and there…Carol MacNeill, John Disley, John Cook, Maude Tiso, Eric Langmuir, Marion MacCormick, Julian and Kate…etc.

On the Eda Fransen

There was a link up with the Cambridge Mountaineering Club here…Chris climbed with them, Peter Steele, Eric Langmuir and John Peacock were presidents at different times.

In 1998 we joined Chris to sail on an old yawl called *'Eda Fransen'* which the Robinsons at Doune on Knoydart had refurbished. As usual all I was asked to supply was some whisky or a few bottles of wine.

I am conscious of the fact that Chris Brasher and John Disley founded the London Marathon in 1981, having been inspired by running in the New York Marathon in 1979. It is perhaps for this, his enthusiasm for orienteering and his Olympic gold medal in 1956, that he is best known. A truly remarkable man. It is very worth mentioning that he and Chris Chataway were the backup that allowed Roger Bannister to run his four-minute mile. Chris once told me that he used to be Chris Chataway's side runner, but then decided he could run faster than Chataway and so started to run for himself and subsequently won a gold!

After Chris died, on 28 February 2003, we held a Memorial Service at Black Sail Hostel in the Lakes to which Chris had given a wind turbine, and where he loved to go and enjoy the famous curries served up by the warden. I could barely believe I was there…in such an

Outside Black Sail Youth Hostel in Lakes

august group…George Lowe and George Band, of Everest fame were there, Joss Naylor the famous Lake District fell runner, and of course Maude, Eric, Marion, the Peacocks, John Cook…Carol.

CHAPTER EIGHT

My family and other Diversions

Camping sauvage in Corsica, 1979

We swooped down over a deep blue sea and spied a dark, forested and brown burnt island, fringed with tiny white bays, and tiny boats like white flecks in blue paint. From Glenmore at 50 degrees to this, 90 degrees, we slurped down the steps from the plane to the tarmac from which a kind of battering heat bounced up at us. After having collected our little Renault Four and piled it full of gear, (Would we really need our down filled sleeping bags?), we made for the nearest beach. Smells accosted us, fennel, oleander and myrtle. As Napoleon said, *"Je la connais par le scent."* Corsica.

Later we camped, and bitterly regretted leaving our Campamats behind (why did we!) as the ground was like iron and we could feel every pine needle through our sleeping bags. Then as the sun sank we heard the chirrup of the cicadas, and had forgotten how, with the disappearance of the heat of the day, these insects open up a nightly chorus, starting slowly until all are chirruping at once!

The days involved many hours spent in the sea. Peter (nine) on the surface, flippers flapping. He spied an octopus peeping out from a crevice and we all had a look at its wonderful camouflage, but failed to tempt it out. Angus, then seven, became brave and even managed to swim underwater, a first for him.

We would spend a few days by the beaches then head inland for some cool, and on this occasion, stopping at a roadside water pipe to hold our heads under the cooling water and soak our hair! Wonderful coolness. Up through rich chestnut forests at Rocca to the Col di Sevi with its domes of blank granite and bare hillsides of dwarf juniper and granite slabs.

There were birds and high trees: Very still, with chaffinches, robins and a tree creeper. Nearby we saw two lesser spotted woodpeckers chasing each other and pecking a tree low down.

We drove over the Col de Vergio, a pass where the Sentier de la Corse, the GR 20, crosses from the Paglia d'Orba to the Lac de Nino side. We packed our bags with tent and food and even the teddies before starting the two and a half hour walk up to the Lac. Through pines and boulders, from lizard to lizard, the boys taking turns to carry the rucksack with the teds. Then we emerged out of the pine trees into the open hillside and the sun, amongst alder bushes with cows, goats, pigs and piglets scuffling amongst the bushes. Finally we came over the ridge to see the lake gleaming blue below us, surrounded by a green meadow where cows grazed, their bells tinkling in the distance. The tent was erected beneath rocks beside the lake, in an attempt to try for some shade. Peter lost no time collecting water boatmen, caddis flies and larvae, as the sun sank and the sky turned a glowing red.

We awoke next morning to the sound of tearing grass, heavy breathing and the tinkling of cowbells. Pigs, sheep and horses were grazing close by. We ate breakfast on the grass then held a pilgrimage round the lake to see French fisherman fishing for small trout with standing rods and salmon eggs. We returned to our tent and tried to fish with cheese and dung worms. Alas, no luck, fussy fish!

Next day we packed and drove to the road end intending to climb Monte Rotondo. We were recommended to take what looked to me to be a horrific path up an almost vertical hillside of rocks, grass and dwarf juniper. There was actually no sign of a path at all!

We started off at six, stumbling upwards through alder bushes, dwarf juniper and another prickly bush. Fred would go on ahead and reconnoitre the route, and we would start again – the boys never complained even though it was truly awful. At 8 p.m. we decided to bivouac rather than descend. Fred went off down to look for water and I set about making a shelter out of the tent under a large rock which slightly overhung a ledge covered with juniper and rocks. The boys who were already in their bags, emerged and put on their boots 'to help Mum', so we collected stones to pin down the tent.

Peter collected a posy for me, "I thought you deserved this, Mum".

Fred was ages. He had gone half way down and we had quite a time heating up the mince in a fierce wind, half under the tent shelter. I poured wine into it and added handfuls of pasta shells. Father returned

with the water. We ate well. The boys even had yogurts. We curled ourselves round one another on top of the prickles and tried to sleep.
Despite being curled round a rock with my head in a cleft I slept surprisingly well. There were stars above us and a fierce wind rose and
then at about six the tent blew off as the rocks had abraded the string it
was tied on with.

We ate a great breakfast of bread and Nutella and drank hot chocolate. We descended…and were glad to wash in a river, and wash out our
dusty clothes, then we camped in a campsite and borrowed a table and
chairs…so we are off the ground at last! There was coffee and the boys
played table football. A lot of children here, all French and with whom
Peter was anxious to communicate, "Bon, bon!"

And so our time continued with wonderful fruits, and swims…
Peter spending hours snorkelling, finding sea urchin shells and tiny
abalone shells with a lovely purple blue sheen inside…Angus helping
with cooking.

Our final excursion was to bivouac, intentionally this time, high up
on the Grande Rondonée below Paglia d'Orba. We found a fantastic site
above a tumbling river and looking over to the Cinque Frati. We were
among tall and untouched pines, juniper bushes and rocks. As Peter
found lizards, butterflies and grasshopper skins, I thought that Gerald
Durrell hardly has a look in! We found a rock with a hollow underneath
and a stone wall round the entrance, which made a perfect sleeping
room. We cut armfuls of bracken for mattresses and built a small
kitchen with stones to sit on and hide our food in.

As we fell asleep we watched bats flying overhead while the moon
shone down on us. A huge pine waved overhead and the occasional
branch snapped as a goat or a cow stepped on it. Clouds scudded past,
then the sky became solid and grey obscuring the summit of Paglia
d'Orba, but in the morning they had cleared to a broken layer of cirrus
and a high wind had risen.

And so we continued down to the coast and our car, ice creams and
a final snorkel, and we headed for home. Fantastic place.

Biking adventures with the boys

NORWAY 1984

Looking back…I can remember bits and pieces…Norway 1984. Peter and I flying to Oslo when he was fourteen, and biking into town, to stay with my friend Bente who helped me with the boys when they were five and six!…Peter had done all the exams necessary and so it seemed the ideal time to take him away from school for a few exciting weeks.

Peter and I had intended to bike north, I think, though plans were pretty non-existent, and had not thought it through at all in terms of distance…totally too much, 'wing and a prayer' comes to mind…so we put the bikes on a train to Bodo, north of the Arctic Circle and then took a boat to the Lofoten Islands…me spending the time on board trying to fix Peter's puncture, actually the tyre was damaged and of a different type to those available in Norway…maybe in Oslo, but not in the far north!

We had a great time, staying in a *Roerbu* at Stamsund, which I visited later when kayaking up there. These are wonderful old fishermen's houses, on stilts over the water. Roar, the warden, ran it, and gave us fish from the harbour. This is cod country and the business up here was huge with cod drying on racks everywhere. I don't think we biked much though I did manage to get a new tyre for Peter.

We then went south on the train, getting off at Dombas and getting a bus to Romsdal as I wanted to see the famous Trolltindwall, which was renowned for climbing at that time. We then picked up our bikes and biked up an unrelenting mountain road to a youth hostel at the top of the Jotunheimen Mountains, Valdresflya (4,658ft). I can remember still Peter persuading me not to give up, as I hauled myself up this terrible ascent. "Come on Mum, you can do it!" Me dying to hitch a lift. Next day we biked down to Fagernes, and I can recall freezing on the bike as we flew so fast downhill. Thirty-one miles and no pedalling. We put the bikes on a bus to Hemsedal to visit someone, then I think we bussed it back to Oslo.

As Norway was so expensive we managed on half an apple a day, and yogurt and frankfurter sausages! It was fun 'managing' on five pounds a day then.

In 1983 we had taken our bikes to Orkney, to see how we enjoyed biking holidays. Orkney was great fun. We stayed in Stromness in the Youth Hostel and biked out to Skara Brae, which was beautiful and deserted. We were sold tickets by a lady with one of those machines that hung on a leather belt over the shoulder, and came out on a paper roll, like bus tickets. On the way back Angus's bike had a burst tyre, so, being mother, I gave him my bike and rode his bike on the rim back to Stromness. It was very tough work! A man in the hostel stripped his leather Levi label off his jeans and patched the tyre! Thereafter we biked to Kirkwall and took a boat out to visit a friend from the Lodge, Reg Popham, who was farming on Sanday. Peter drove the tractor as we took in hay. A very happy time with Reg and his kids.

Shetland was very different. In 1985, my friend, Sally, and I took our children on the boat to Lerwick. I remember the Shetland Football team was returning victorious and were in cheery form. We danced and laughed and the journey passed very quickly.

We did feel a bit stuck with bikes, as it took too long to get any-where! It rained almost constantly, as we headed south, to a fish factory at Scalloway and on down to Mousa, where we visited the famous Broch, the only one untouched by people pinching the stones for build-ing. Beautiful place. We tended to stop at bus shelters and upturned boat 'huts' where we brewed up on our gas stove, out of the rain, before proceeding further. We managed to visit St Ninian's Isle and then headed back to the hostel at Lerwick to have a rethink. We couldn't make it to Herma Ness for the birds, just too far. But we did get to Fetlar, but saw no snowy owl, and to my friend, Penny, at Baltasound on Unst, who took us in and was very good to us all…wet and a bedrag-gled as we were. We were re-energised by this.

Biking south again to Lerwick it upset me to see so many Shetland ponies and foals, destined to become dog meat. Twelve pounds for a pony. I wanted go buy them all.

DENMARK 1987

Sally, Ben, Angus, Peter and I set off with our bikes to cross to Esbjerg. It was very rough so mother was sick then departed for her bunk, not to be seen again that night. We had a week biking in the southern part of

Denmark, and Peter's diary recalls endless trucks, but also a hedgehog poking its nose thru the spokes of his bike. We shared the most light and delicious Danish pastries, like nothing I ever ate in the UK, and the boys would buy them with their pocket money and share them, which was very generous. We had punctures and torn tyres, went through four tubes and a new tyre.

The best part was a day spent on the island of Aeroskobing in the south, where we had only one road and visited a Bottle Ship collection of 1,700 bottles collected and made up by 'Bottle Peter'! We seemed to live on frankfurters and potatoes and eggs, and because were put in 'family rooms' as we were mothers and children, well Peter was seventeen, we had a rough time with snoring. I seem to remember spending nights sleeping under the tables in the dining room, (Peter, one hour in toilet!) and Peter wrote: *"route planning in progress, now got three ulcers."* But we visited churches, and biked into Legoland, and then pushed, against a head wind and rain, towards Esbjerg and our ferry: *"lunch leaning against someone's hedge, out of force 6 wind"*... and visited a Sofartsmuseum, which we enjoyed and then rolled along confidently towards our boat, which we thought sailed at 7 p.m. We did wonder why all the cars were loaded and then discovered it sailed at 6 p.m., we only just made it! Swallowing a lot of seasick pills I joined the others in gobbling down a massive feast of pickled herring, caviar, prawns, salmon, chicken. Then it was such a rough night that I found out later Angus had slept on the top deck in the lounge, not wanting to risk going below.

CHAPTER NINE
Further Adventures

Sailing

While I was married we bought a beautiful boat, a Warrior 35, with help from the Tourist Board who were giving money to people who would put their boats out for charter. They were trying to encourage tourists to Scotland. We called her *'Sickle Moon'* after the mountain overlooking the one we climbed in India in 1969. When Fred and I took delivery of her in about 1975 we sailed her through the Crinan Canal. I got into terrible trouble for not steering her accurately enough and risking her new hull on the walls of the Canal. It was only later, when we made it through, we discovered that the steering mechanism had not been bolted together. We had many sailing trips on the west coast with the boys and friends and my last trip was to sail from Ullapool to Roscoff in France. We meant to sail to the Azores but the weather was dreadful. So bad that we took the inner route through the Irish Sea, where we had a force 7 storm, and crawled into Holyhead. We had water in the bilges and I had been totally sick for five days. But we did recover and sail her south accompanied by more storms. Off the Scillies in the dark we had no chart (having meant to sail to the Azores!), so that Fred wanted us, rightly, to stay off the land until daylight. He was overruled. And we sailed her in. We had a terrifying approach talked in by a guy at a barbecue: *"look for the green buoy to port"* etc., where we saw no buoy. We made it. We sailed across the Channel to Roscoff in France and then to Guernsey from where I flew home to look after my boys.

The GR20, 2003

In Corsica. I had holidayed with the boys there but now decided to do the famous GR20, which runs the length of the island. This seems to be variously described as *'Europe's toughest trail'* or *'two weeks of rock climbing without ropes'*. I was ready and fit. But there was one section on which I wanted moral support. The Cirque de la Solitude. This is a rocky section on day four which descends 656ft, all rock, to a ledge from where one climbs out with the help of unreliable chains to get back on the 'path'. I found a friend, Mike Atherton, to come with me, which was wonderful. It is a very tough trek, mostly on rock. I carried just a flysheet, a sheet of nylon to cover the ground, and a lightweight sleeping bag. One has to camp near the huts from which one can buy wine in old bottles and perhaps a loaf of bread if the warden has been to the valley recently. I bought one, and it was like a brick! He also sells pasta and tomato sauce which I ate daily, and cooked this on the communal gas rings I found at the sites. I met a lot of French people who would check on me if I failed to arrive, as my friend descended fairly frequently to the valley to see his wife. He pulled out at Vizzavona and I did the last five days on my own. It is easier from here. Less rock scrambling. Great trip. Wonderful views to a tantalising blue Mediterranean and marvellous campsite at Lac de Nino. which I had visited with the family 24 years before!

Sea Kayaking

Scotland

Boats on beach

Going round the south end of Eilean nan Ron, I turned the boat to face the green wall of surf coming towards me, "Oh shit". I am overturned. Terrifying spot. Behind me cliffs, all around me rocks, swept by ever crashing surf. But I had support. I was part of a group kayaking on the edge of the Pentland Firth. Having been there before in a climbing environment I knew the emotions. But here I could drown. I looked at a sea swept rock and thought I could sit on it if all else failed, but it would not have worked. My two instructors came to my rescue.

Speed was of the essence. I held on to my boat, lay on my back and kicked…Pete towed me off, then the other instructor clipped on too and both pulled as I swam. It was a serious place. Finally I managed to climb back into my boat, with Pete pulling me over into the cockpit. Someone gave me a Kit Kat when we landed round the corner and I changed into dry clothes. Later, Pete said to me, "M.A., we thought we might not manage to pull you off"…but they did.

Having put it to the staff at the Centre that maybe this week on the North Coast, on the edge of the Pentland Firth, was too hard for me and that I was making a fool of myself trying to participate, I went. The two leaders had discussed it and decided that I would manage and could keep to the edge in 'difficult' spots. (To be fair, I think I had a reputation with them for being tough and liking challenges.)

We drove north and on the way stopped at the harbour at Sarclet, just south of Wick. Climbing out of the cosy Transit van, I saw the water in the wide open harbour. Choppy stuff. There seemed no point in wondering. On with the gear, buoyancy jacket, spray deck, "Oh help that's my boat, I am next". As the launch is difficult off a steep shell bank, they launched me. I did not want to go. I had not noticed that the paddle blade was set at the wrong angle, so that when I went for support stroke (when flat blade should slap the water surface) I got a slice and the paddle went down into the water. It was a miracle I stayed upright. I followed in a daze as the group ventured out into the North Sea swell. 20 to 30ft troughs…crazy…a wee figure would disappear up the side and over the top of a massive wave…but once out on the North Sea swell I was committed, no turning round and going back. Far too difficult. It was like paddling over the Pentlands, I was on automatic pilot, paddling over waves 30ft high.

Next day Duncansby Head. This is the spot on the top right hand side of the map of Scotland and is very exposed. Lovely morning up a coast of stunning cliffs, geos, and arches…then the Head. We waited in a little geo at the side, till the tide races started…like the Spey in flood… All bravado, I paddled forward and out into the stream. Frantically driving myself forward I came out of the rapid at the top saying, "Fucking awful, not doing that again!" I hid in an eddy behind the stack, (The Knee). I was balancing on a boiling and moving eddy… then tried the race again, and couldn't cope so paddled out backwards but upright…then it came down other side, and huge surfing waves… weird which I just watched…from my moving eddy. Trying to stay upright, it's like sitting on top of a vertical jet of water.

Next day we crossed to the island of Stroma in the flood tide…I was last and Pete said, "M.A., if you capsize here you will end up in Norway". Light bulb moment. The water was moving so fast. I could not catch up with the rest. I was worn out, and my arms did not seem to be delivering any power. My technique was wrong. No rotation. Suddenly I noticed this steel spike moving sideways in the water, and couldn't understand how it could shift so cleanly when it was fixed to the sea floor. Houses on the island moved left too and with terrifying clarity I saw it was me being taken sideways. Towards Norway! Pete had said that the tide was moving at nine knots! I paddled harder…At times like this I won't let my mind wander to my status as a mother and grandmother. Somehow that is part of another life. In the modern idiom, perhaps I compartmentalise.

My sea kayaking started late, after I had instructed white water kayaking and had my ration of adventures there, including taking a group from Fort William to Inverness, camping for a week. My boys were on that trip too. Then some days of Canadian canoeing and a wonderful trip I led down the River Spey, camping en route, and ending in what is always the magic moment of coming to where the sea laps the river.

Magic memories are of kayaking round the whole collection of islands south of Barra, scaring myself silly going down the west side of Mingulay and through a tunnel, where water gushed in from the side from a hidden passage. All dark. The swell trying to take me up against the cliffs. Camping on Mingulay above the dunes as puffins waddled past to find their burrows, and being blessed with a flat sea to paddle across the notorious passages between Pabbay and Sandray, we went gleefully forth. "Oh look, yet another basking shark," the cries rang out as one after another a dorsal fin knifed the surface and broke their cover. One swam under my boat in the bay at Mingulay as we left the island. A portent of what was to come. They do have huge mouths but I am told that they do not eat meat.

I enjoyed magic times paddling off Orkney, and Skye and terrifying times on a 'following sea' where the front of the boat rises up on the crest of a wave and threatens to turn you over into the trough. I hated those times. Some people love them and surf the waves. I am not good enough. Lorne was full of magic and sparkling seas and the days round the Summer Isles were magic. Places I had only heard of, and then I had been there. Paddling round Handa, with all the birds sitting on the water in rafts, and along the Moray Coast below Troup Head where the gannets threaten to drop their guano on your head. One of my favourite

Cuillins and Skye

areas has to be near Arisaig, so many seals nosing out of the water in curiosity, and their big Labrador eyes watching you from behind. The views across to Eigg, Rum and Skye of blue, blue sea with rugged outlines against the sky must vie with any other to be the best sea view in Scotland.

In the Land of the Midnight Sun

In the summer of 2011, I fulfilled a dream to paddle in the Lofoten Islands in the land of the Midnight Sun. These islands sit off the North West coast of Norway, about a hundred miles north of the Arctic Circle. Fay and I had gone out a week early and spent a happy time in an old fisherman's house or *Roerbu*, which was now a youth hostel near Stamsund. We had travelled north from Oslo by overnight train to Bodo and could feel the country changing as we ventured north. Fay stayed awake all night to watch the changing terrain, and the moment we crossed the Arctic Circle. We then took the Hurtigruten coastal ferry across the Vestfjorden to Stamsund. This daily boat travels up the coast from Bergen to Kirkenes, taking six days to visit thirty-five ports on the way.

The islands spread their tall, craggy physique against the sky, the blackness tinted with infinite shades of green and yellow. Of course there is no night! We are in the land of the Midnight Sun. We had a happy week, renting bikes from the warden to explore, and taking a local bus to the village of Å at the bottom of the island group. The warden, Roar, had been there since 1975, and must have been there when, in 1984, I took my son biking and we had stayed in this *Roerbu*. One night Roar took me into one of his sheds and dipped into his freezer and pulled out a bag of frozen cod. It was delicious. The Lofoten Islands have long been known to hang cod from racks to dry. Indeed cod fishing was the mainstay of the island economy. Each winter when the waters of the Gulf Stream and the Arctic Ocean meet, the cod come down from the Barents Sea (north coast of Russia) to spawn. The main industry is stockfish, when the fish have their heads removed, are then tied together round their tails and hung outside to dry on big A frames. Around 16 million kilogramme of cod are hung up to dry here each year – in 1947 the total was 146 million kilogramme. A lot of these dried fish end up in Italy. Think Lofoten, think cod!

Six of us assembled on the campsite in Svolvaer and were issued with our lunch bags. The leader had been shopping and bought the food for the week. Each of us was given a carrier bag with lunch. A packet of Ryvita, four cereal bars, five pieces of fruit, some cheese, and jam. Was that really all? The cheese was scoffed in two days. I rationed myself to four slices of Ryvita a day, one when we arrived in camp. Ryvita and jam is not very satisfying after a hard morning paddling.

But it was a good week. We paddled north up the long inner channel, the Raftsundet, until we emerged at the top end and out of the fjord onto the north coast near Hadselfjorden. On our way north we had ventured into the Trollfjorden, a very deep and narrow fjord, which is visited by the Hurtigruten, and a seaplane flew in while we were there. A highlight would have been to see the ferry turn around at the end with the help of side thrusters. But our leader was for off, so we had to go. I was disappointed in the lack of wildlife. No seals, no otters, just a lot of white tailed eagles sitting at strategic points on rocks. When we did come out of the cold, dark fjord at the islands, we saw lots of seabirds. I think, like me, they found the blackness of the deep water too extreme and hostile. We saw terns and puffins, and made sure to keep our camp at the far end of the beach and away from the oystercatcher's nest and eggs. There were sheep on the island, and the leader of the flock wore a bell.

Returning south our leader told us we might even find a 'café'…a café wow! We paddled with enthusiasm, our tummies rumbling, for in the fjords it is beautifully pristine, with just rocks and trees and no shops! *Digermulen.* We scrambled out of our kayaks, nearly falling into the water in our haste. No café. But it was a Co-op and in this part of Norway the Co-ops have a thermos of coffee by the checkout. Life was looking up. We pushed the door open, and to our left we saw shelf upon shelf of donuts, pecan bars and bread. We fell on them. We bought hard cheese and blue cheese. We staggered out and collapsed on the grass for our feast. This, the shortage of food at lunch, was the downside to our holiday and actually it is the part we all remember the most for we did paddle long distances and at times it was indeed relentless, covering over 81 miles in the week.

Unfortunately, we could not see the midnight sun, as we were in a fjord, which obscured the horizon. Though one night at the island we caught a cloud free night and had a glimpse of a sunset. We took the Hurtigruten to Bodo from Svolvaer, and suddenly I realised that the boat seemed to be tilting. Everyone was on the starboard side watching a pod of Orcas playing in the Vestfjorden. A good end.

Elafiti Islands and Croatia

This was a luxurious week of kayaking in the sun, swimming in warm water, eating out in good restaurants and enjoying grilled squid. We visited Lopud first then moved to Sipan. We had flown to Dubrovnik and taken the ferry to Lopud, where we dined in the guesthouse owner's orchard, using her home made olive oil and eating the fresh fruit.

An easy week though we did cover 62 miles on the water.

Scuba diving at the Red Sea

Socialising with the fish, a few scares being buddied up with the wrong person and going too deep. But I loved the fish and 'the deep blue'.

Photography

I studied for three years in Edinburgh and to my surprise was awarded a gold award! But there was no future in this for me. Too late?

St Kilda

The Street and sheep

Who does not dream of crossing the seas, 40 miles off Harris, to view Boreray, the Stacs and Hirta, the collection of islands called St Kilda? I had thought about it for a while and volunteered to work with the National Trust there in 2014, it happened to coincide with Peter chartering a boat for the same dates, also with my desire to get to St Kilda. I had a happy time with the National Trust after a truly awful journey over there. I was so sick I couldn't walk!

I dug out ditches and painted the 'gun' which had been installed there in 1918 after a German U Boat did, in fact, shell the area round Village Bay. According to reports just the manse, church and jetty storehouse were damaged and one lamb was killed, "The cattle having run off when the shelling began". The gun was never fired.

The group was fun and we explored the island and had merry times with the local lambs cavorting past. But for me the best bit was seeing Peter sailing in to Village Bay with his friends on '*Sleat Lady*'. He took me on the boat round the island with Helen, our cook. Magic.

Also we got close to the gannets on Stac Lee. It's an amazing place, with no television or radio or phones and just the sound of the sheep. A very special time.

Antarctica, 2016

St Andrews Bay

I had long wanted to go 'South'. I had read much about Shackleton and Scott, and my son, plus many of my friends, had worked down there, so when I sold my house and had the funds I decided to go.

I chose to go with Naturetrek. They had elected to take us on Ortelius, a ship that carries 100 people, which is small by Antarctic standards and ensured we would not be crowded and would have many landings. The Ortelius is Polish but owned and run by Oceanwide Expeditions.

It's a long way from Edinburgh to Ushuaia. In fact it was 48 hours of travelling with three flights, and a break in Buenos Aires where, clutching a packed lunch, we all went birding.

After a buffet dinner and wine we all collapsed, however some folk were up at seven the next morning for a bird walk. Not me. But we had a few hours in the Tierra del Fuego National Park, with its native *Nothofagus antarctica* trees which are similar to beeches, and a stunning coastal walk although we failed to see the Magellanic Woodpecker.

We joined our boat that afternoon and sailed. We had lectures on lifeboat drill and where we would eat and have our talks etc. I swallowed some pills and got ready for the first sail to the Falklands. Half way through a talk on penguins I disappeared down the three flights to my bed, in a cabin I shared with two sisters. These three flights dominated the trip, as it was always three flights up for a coffee or a talk or to go on deck to see the birds and the whales, and when the boat was unsteady it became even harder to pull oneself up by the banisters.

But we landed on Saunders Island at the Falklands to a reception committee of Magellanic penguins. I will not forget that. Our Zodiac rubber boat landed us all and we wandered amongst Gentoo penguins, feeding their young or lying flat asleep, and a small colony of King Penguins. It was magic. There was an Albatross colony up the hill, but I did not think my ankle would take that, and did not go.

Our next landing was at Stanley to put ashore someone who had cracked a rib as he fell while on the boat. Poor man, but we did enjoy a stroll in this famous place, viewing a terrace of Victorian bay-windowed houses in Philomel Street! Back on board we hoovered our

Boat and Gentoo penguins

182

clothes and rucksacks before our next landing, having already dipped our wellies in disinfectant on deck.

Thereafter we sailed south for two days accompanied by black browed albatross, which have a wingspan of eight feet, to the Shag Rocks, and then South Georgia itself. A wonderful, wild mountainous place, with glaciers and the remains of three whaling stations, Stromness, Husvik and Leith, rotting and rusted by the shores, adding drama of the past to the present stark beauty. At Grytviken we learnt that 46,000 whales had been processed, all that remains are rusting boats and oil tanks. We landed there to pay homage at Shackleton's grave. We toasted him with Famous Grouse before we posted cards home. Mine arrived six weeks later, so it didn't go on the back of an albatross after all.

We then landed at St Andrews Bay with over 400,000 King penguins along the beach against a backdrop of mountains and glaciers. Totally mind-blowing. The noise was indescribable. Some were swimming, or feeding chicks, fat brown babies, which must moult and be fat and ready for winter when it comes, soon. Fur Seals are to be treated with caution and respect. Very fair given that they are so territorial. But I forgot about them when I was photographing a sunrise on the beach at 4 a.m., and lay down to get a better photograph of the penguins silhouetted against the sky. I did not see a fur seal approaching from behind with his teeth bared!

Heading south we cruised into Drygalski Fjord, which was spectacular, and very like a Norwegian fjord with cliffs and hanging glaciers. Then it was off to the open sea, the infamous Southern Ocean. Lots of whales were seen blowing, some good 'tails' when they dived. A wandering albatross followed alongside us and we also saw petrels and a few prions. Lots of icebergs.

This was a long sail, broken by meals, and talks and the film of Shackleton. These were three long days and we did not land at the South Orkneys as planned as the forecast was bad and we had to be back in Ushuaia for planes. In bad weather the boat has to slow down. It was pitching all over the place. Peter was tracking me back home in Scotland and saw we had changed course before I knew!

We had a short landing at Paulet Island, just off the Peninsula and south of Dundee Island, a volcanic island with russet and grey shale on

King Penguins in South Georgia

the hillside. I sat amongst the Adelie penguins on the beach and watched them pecking ice for fresh water. We tried to land on the Peninsula but the captain said there was too much ice, so we went up the Antarctic Sound for the night. Next day it was decided we could land, at a point called Cape Green, off the Tabarin Peninsula. There was

M.A. at 60 deg South

a lot of brash ice, floating bits amongst broken up pack ice. Ten Zodiacs set off. Finding their way through this to the land. It was very exciting and more so for one lot who, on the way back, sprang a puncture in their boat, but as the air is compartmentalised, they were fine, but did transfer to another boat. A leopard seal was lying out on the pack. We were lucky to see him, although he is an ugly beast, *'the shark of the Southern Ocean'*.

We headed up Antarctic Sound, called Iceberg Alley, and across Bransfield Strait to the South Shetland Islands where we made for Half Moon Bay. A stunning place of snow and mountains and lots of Chinstrap penguins.

Thereafter it was two days, and more pills, back north across Drake Passage to Cape Horn, which I discovered is the actually southernmost island in a collection of islands. It was very misty and dull.

Another day up the Beagle Channel, being met by a pilot to escort us in, and we are back in Ushuaia. Sitting by a cruise ship disgorging 2,000 passengers, we felt glad to be small. And it's over! Hugely memorable trip!

South Shetland islands

Chinstrap penguins

Epilogue

My story is finished thus far. Up to this point, where a new life may begin – a different life. I look back at where I have been and the people whose paths I have crossed. The Tibetans whose lives have been changed for ever by their land being annexed by China. I read about Tibet sixty years ago and have no idea why, but the fascination with that land, and the story of the Dalai Lama escaping over the mountains has stayed with me. I am happiest in wild empty places and was fortunate to have visited Tibet several times.

I visited many places where poverty is the norm. Perhaps Bolivia was the hardest for me. The mountain people there lived on dried potatoes all year. They would preserve them by freezing them in ponds, then, later, they would pound them into flour. This happened in the cold mountains, where their only covering was ragged old clothes. I was wearing a down jacket. I began to feel uncomfortable travelling with a group, with warm clothes and expensive cameras and tents and even a cook crew, when one of our items if sold would keep these people alive for a year. I did not like it.

I was lucky. I have also fulfilled my dreams of going to the Antarctic and to Namibia, so I have really lived in both the areas of privilege and deprivation. I hope I have learned that we are all one people in the world and to appreciate what we have.

The future worries me for my children and my grandchildren. We are not caring for our planet. Greed seems to govern many nations. Even the krill in the Antarctic are being syphoned out of the sea by huge ships. Obviously this deprives the whales and other creatures of a precious food source. Closer to home, we have wind farms sprouting up over wild land. Nature is beaten into submission.

But we continue to hope. We must be positive and do our best to preserve wildness in our beautiful land.

> *"Meanwhile the wild geese, high in the clean blue air,*
> *   are heading home again.*
> *Whoever you are, no matter how lonely,*
> *the world offers itself to your imagination,*
> *calls to you like the wild geese, harsh and exciting –*
> *over and over announcing your place in the family of things."*

from *Wild Geese* by Mary Oliver

Appendix: Munro diary

SECTION 1: LOCH LOMOND TO LOCH TAY

Ben Lomond. Penultimate. (17 Aug 95) Marjorie Langmuir

Stunning day. Lots of punters commented endlessly on our walking poles, "No snow yet" etc. Leant on trig point, until realised it was full of wasps. At loch stripped off and swam, then jumped off the pier.

Ben Vorlich and Ben Vane (July 94) Helen Geddes 7 hours

Relentless up to Ben Vorlich thru outcrops, long ridge (2.5hrs) and vertical descent down, then vertical ascent up to Ben Vane. Thunder rolling, pouring rain and thick mist. Muddy tramp down path to car. Legs pretty sore, beer in Killin and fish supper in Aberfeldy. Home 11.30 p.m. Good day, best part I don't have to do them ever again! "Seven to go".

Beinn Chabhair (April 94) Isobel 5.5 hours

In rain and gales, gave it a go. Bog, bog, bog. Gales, 80 mph gusts, on hands and knees. Did it. Absolutely shattered. "Hardest Munro I have done". (No. 263)

SECTION 2: LOCH TAY TO RANNOCH MOOR

First I climbed Ben Vorlich and Stuc a'Chroin (Oct 85) Solo, south of Loch Earn, and set off for home. But the moon was full, so I turned round near Loch Tay and at 5.30 p.m. began ascent of **Ben Lawers**. At times I was walking in moonlight, other times in the deep disturbing shadow of the hill. Sat on top at 8.30 p.m. and ate a Penguin. Looked at lights below on Loch Tay and was glad I had foregone my woodwork class! Fantastic experience to be so alone in the dark on the mountain. Lights in cottages below.

Creag Mhor and Beinn Heasgarnich (July 91) Ian Forder

Lashing rain, thunder and lightning for three hours, but day outweighed by car dying, joining AA at Ballinluig and getting to bed, after a series of tows up the A9, at 3 a.m.!

Beinn Achaladair and B a'Chreachain (April 93) Solo

Tennis elbow, Achilles tendon, sore knee and tight boots…what a wreck. Very hot, made silly errors coming down and had to traverse rocky slopes numb feet and tight boots, a killer. Car keys and Orangina saved the day. Could hardly walk across tarmac to pay for petrol in FW.

SECTION 3: STRATH ORCHY TO GLEN COE

Beinn Eunaich and a' Chochuill (Sept 91) Marjorie, Alan Keegan 5 hours

Very warm day, no wind. Wonderful views in all directions, Rum, Skye, Paps of Jura. (12 hours from Aviemore)

Ben Cruachan solo 9 hours

Great day…had post office dog with me. Met Kenny (Welder from Glasgow) who was a Kevin Costner lookalike, could I be so lucky! Walked together and he melted snow to make me tea…had eggs stored in a Vitalite box. Nearly shared a bottle of wine, but I went home…he remarked it had been "a bitter sweet day"!

Ben Starav etc (June 91) solo 8 hours

Started with Helen Geddes but she was not feeling great and went down, but told me to go on. High cumulus, blue sky, sun and views all round. Paps of Jura, the Ben, Ben Cruachan, Schiehallion etc. Really ran it, lovely ridge. Met guy on top who had done Island Peak in Nepal with Classic Nepal! Arrived shattered at car park to find Helen on one side and Hamish Brown on other! He gave me orange juice. Most welcome. Dipped in Allt Mheuran.

Creise, Meall a Bhuiridh, Stob Ghabhar and Stob a' Choire Odhair (June 91) Helen Geddes. 9 hours

Stayed Blackrock Cottage. Got wrong hill to start with...mixed weather. Frogs, lizard, super flowers, hare. Visited Hamish McInnes.

SECTION 4: LOCH LINNHE TO LOCH ERICHT

Mamores to Sgor an Iubhair (May 88) solo 12 hours

Very windy, on hands and knees sometimes. So left out Stob Ban and Mullach nan Coirean and will have to go back, bother!

Grey Corries, Aonach Beag and Aonach Mor (May 88) solo 11.5 hours

Great weather, lots of snow, especially on last two. Met two people on Stob Coire Easain. Decided to keep going as was up there already, and would save me going back! Very tired legs and awful steep descent from Aonach Mor into glen below and dreadful trek back by forest fence to car at Fersit.

Beinn na Lap then cup of tea at Loch Ossian YH and did Carn Dearg and Sgor Gaibhre (Aug 86) solo 10 hours

Walked in over B na Lap...came to YH, lots of folk sitting at tables... had cup of tea, made my bed, then set off and did some more! Beautiful evening. Next day took train out, and Warden came after me on his motorbike with my thermos.

Ben Alder (July 89) with Peter 7 hours

Rang George Oswald who was head keeper on the Estate and he gave me key to the gate up past Loch Ericht. Put car in shed near Loch Pattack. "If you don't do that the horses will eat the wing mirrors!" Great day, very hot, clegs. Drank lots of water, swam in river and drank cool lagers out of loch!

SECTION 5: DRUMOCHTER MOUNTAINS

Meall Cuaich (82) Marjorie

Other three (84 and 85) solo

SECTION 6: THE GRAMPIANS, BLAIR ATHOLL TO BRAEMAR

Beinn a' Ghlo (84) solo

Carn a' Chlamain (89) solo

Seven miles walk in or two pounds to drive in. Met guy on summit who had come from Brussels for the weekend.

Cairnwell, Carn a' Gheoidh and Carn Aosda (89) solo 8.5 hours

SECTION 7: THE MOUNTH, GLEN SHEE TO LOCHNAGAR

Glas Maol…and seven Munros, total (May 89) solo 8.5 hours.

Easy walking, found a dunlin's nest. Helped a hang glider to launch his kite off Glas Maol. Byeee.

Lochnagar to Broad Cairn (June 87) solo 8 hours

Thick mist. Did five Munros…went back with Alan and Marjorie in '96 to see it!

Mount Keen (92) Helen

Biked in and out. Nice day.

SECTION 8: THE CAIRNGORM MOUNTAINS

Close to home these mountains seem to have attracted less attention from me...my backyard really...but one long day does spring to mind, 12 hrs 40 mins to walk into **Beinn a Bhuird** from Glenmore, and back. Starting out with Hamish who was on the TGO walk across Scotland.

Record walking to **Derry Cairngorm** topless...in heat...saw a Ptarmigan chick...and swam in Spey when got back, with Angus, who jumped off the bridge.

SECTION 9: THE MONADHLIATH AND CREAG MEAGAIDH

Geal Charn with Jules Lines.

SECTION 10: GLEN SHIEL

Ladhar Bheinn *'one of the finest mountains in Scotland, with narrow rocky ridges, spectacular carries and a seascape setting which makes the views from it, or towards it, among the best in the land'*. Did this mountain many times also with clients on my *Freespirit* walking weeks.

One of my favourite areas, I always left one to go back for. But Kintail boasts the South Cluny Ridge (my first big Munro day with Marjorie and Ann Wakeling...my best memory is of it being very hot and Ann and I stripped off, only to surprise a man behind the summit cairn on Creag a Mhaim!) This was 1982 and probably kick-started my Munros.

SECTION 11: GLEN AFFRIC AND KINTAIL

The hills up past Loch Arkaig were always dreaded. The road was narrow and had lots of ups and downs and I usually ended up lying on the grass for a few minutes to recover.

SECTION 12: GLEN CANNICH TO GLEN CARRON

This area not totally memorable except for a long day with Sally Hayes, one with Peter and one with Helen Geddes.

SECTION 13: THE TORRIDON MOUNTAINS

Great hills, with Marjorie and Peter and a solo traverse of Beinn Eighe.

SECTION 14: LOCH MAREE TO THE FANNAICHS

Have very little memory of these days...apart from walking alone across the Fannichs in thick mist and meeting two guys who told me to be careful of navigation! Also climbed the **Fisherfield Six** in 11 hours with Pete Surfleet and ended up at Shenavall Bothy in front of a roaring fire and clasped a dram, offered by a couple drying socks, while Pete went upstairs to cook our pasta!

Also climbed **An Teallach** with Fred and found the pinnacles 'a bit scary'. Fantastic hill.

SECTIONS 15 AND 16: BEN WYVIS TO BEN HOPE

Biked in from the north to climb Seana Braigh...one of the most 'distant Munros occupying a remote, lofty cliff girt situation in true wilderness country'...Peter and Marjorie joined me on 'the Deargs', and Marjorie and I had a superb traverse of Ben More Assent, one very hot day when the deer were lying on snow patches to cool off and their young were calling their mothers. We had some trouble hitching back for our car!

Did Ben Hope with Fred in 1972!

SECTION 17: THE ISLANDS OF MULL AND SKYE

And with that short title we dismiss some terrifying 'Munro bagging' on the Skye Ridge. The weather superb, Marjorie and I set off for Ben More on Mull, only to find we had no money for the ferry at Lochaline, but we conned our way on. Great day, we saw a sea eagle and on our way down an owl flew over us, herons everywhere. On ferry on way back offered to send money, but they said no...too much trouble...!

On Skye I slept in the car, then went off at 7 a.m. to climb **Am Basteir** and along ridge to **Sgurr nan Gillean**...enjoyed so much climbing on gabbro. Diary records very sore toes. Probably swollen feet on a hot day.

Big day on **Sgurr a Mhaidaidh** when I wimped out of continuing along the ridge to do **Sgurr na Banachdich** so that I retraced my steps to the road and reascended from Coire na Banachdich!

Sgurr Mhic Choinnich took two attempts, the first in 1994 when was on ridge itself and rock was damp, but returned in 1995 one very hot evening. Diary records: *"found it very airy, and quite shaky but just looked at ground and rock ahead. Ate five Dextrose on top to steady my nerves, didn't look at plaque on cairn, to someone who died"*…it drops a long way down both sides. I met Julian Lines in the campsite, and bats flew past my tent.

Yes, I did do the **In Pin**…with Dennis Gray, in 1964!!

Acknowledgements

To the following who helped me with diary extracts, support and information, without whom it would have been even harder.

John Leonard	Kailash
Roger Hoyle	Kailash
John Rosenfield	History of Loch Morlich Youth Hostel and the Kompagnie Linge
Hamish Brown	Morocco and Munros
Myrtle Simpson	General encouragement
Harry Jamieson	Skiing in Scotland
Rob Collister	Matterhorn and Kenya
Fay Brown	Sea kayaking
Peter Harper	General and Antarctica
Peter Steele	Acute Mountain Sickness
Albert Chapman	Dolpo
Raymond Fawcett	Dolpo
Jules Lines	Encouragement and check-ups
Robert Macfarlane	Mountains of the Mind
Wilfred Noyce	South Col (by kind permission of Random House)

and to Tommy Dunbar for digitalising all my slides, Kath Hamper for initial proof reading and the staff of the Edinburgh Apple store for their support.

The most enormous thanks must go to Janet McLeman (Granite) who took on the role of editor early on and encouraged and supported me for years and made me keep going. Without her help the book would simply not have happened!

All photographs by the author unless otherwise credited.